A	B	C	D	E	F	G	H
A72 AC1							

I	J	K	L	M	N	P	Q
		80 KA15	69		c16 O14S	P.SA	

SPECIAL NEEDS UNIT 01902 55625 6

The Spade as Mighty as the Sword

'And he gave it for his opinion, "that whoever could make two ears of corn, or two blades of grass, to grow upon a spot of ground where only one grew before, would deserve better of mankind, and do more essential service to his country, than the whole race of politicians put together."'

— Jonathan Swift, *Gulliver's Travels*

The Spade as Mighty as the Sword

THE STORY OF THE
SECOND WORLD WAR
'DIG FOR VICTORY' CAMPAIGN

DANIEL SMITH

First published 2011 by
Aurum Press Limited
7 Greenland Street
London NW1 0ND
www.aurumpress.co.uk

A catalogue record for this book is available from the British Library.

ISBN 978 1 84513 617 8

1 3 5 7 9 10 8 6 4 2
2011 2013 2015 2014 2012

Typeset in Perpetua by Eclipse, Chelmsford, Essex

Printed and bound in Great Britain by
MPG Books, Bodmin, Cornwall

CONTENTS

1. 'He that Tilleth …'

On 19 March 1941, a woman by the name of Joan Strange updated her personal diary (subsequently published as *Despatches from the Home Front*). 'Help! I've not written this old diary for nearly a week,' she wrote. 'It's the allotment's fault! The weather has been so good that I've gone up most evenings and get too tired digging to write the diary.'

Joan was a member of one of the British nation's essential fighting forces, waging a daily battle on what was to become known as the 'Garden Front'. Through dint of hard work, frugality and inventiveness, Joan and millions of others like her ensured the nation remained sated during the Second World War. No longer able to guarantee the international imports on which the nation had for too long relied for its food, the British government had set about persuading its people to live off the fat of its own land. Those not fighting on the front lines took up the challenge with gusto, joining an army of growers united by the clarion call 'Dig for Victory'. The authorities hoped the campaign would help the United Kingdom avoid the food shortages that almost proved so catastrophic during the First World War, while boosting levels of nutrition and morale amongst the public, and freeing up shipping for other vital supplies instead.

Joan herself had grown up in Worthing during the First World War and was a most eager horticulturalist by the time of the Second World War. But even as hardy a grower as she occasionally felt the strain. On 3 May 1941 she noted: 'For four weeks I have had acute neuritis in my right arm thanks to "digging for victory" in the north-east wind in the evening!' However, as any good gardener will attest to, there are always rewards for the pain and toil. A mere month later, her joy was apparent as the first crops emerged: 'The allotment is looking wonderful and I cut 2 lb of spinach today – the first fruits!' Through such efforts the Diggers for Victory would harvest a million tons of produce per year at the campaign's peak.

Within the space of eighteen months at the start of the war, the campaign helped reconfigure the national landscape and the lives of its citizens. In villages and towns up and down the country, every available scrap of spare land was given over to the cause. Lawns, flower beds, parks and playing fields, tennis courts, railway sidings, window boxes, even the grass verges at the side of the road – all were turned over to food production. In a 2006 Royal Horticultural Society documentary on the campaign, one contributor called Fred Ferebee remembered returning to his family home in Southwark after a period in the country as an evacuee:

> I got back home and noticed some amazing changes ... The biggest change was in the small back garden ... Dad had changed everything bar one rose over a trellis which he loved ... And everywhere was planted with runner beans and peas and tomatoes, lettuce, everything you could imagine.

The government reported in 1942 that over half of all households were growing at least some of their own veg. Men, women and children of all backgrounds pooled their efforts. Sunday afternoon was a particularly popular time to get the veg patch straight, though many more hours besides were spent cultivating and nurturing. Even the church got in on the act, delivering messages of encouragement to the amateur grower from the pulpit. Oft used as the starting point of such sermons was Proverbs 28:19: 'He that tilleth his land shall have plenty of bread'. Bread and much more, in fact! One Kent schoolboy reminisced on the 'excitement of digging small carrots on the allotment, selecting one, cleaning it on my sleeve and biting into its fresh crispness!'

The pleasure in success was only heightened by the physical dangers under which growers laboured. Herbert Brush of Forest Hill reported in his diary on 26 October 1940 (quoted in *Our Longest Days* by Sandra Koa Wing) on the impact of a German bombing raid: '... I went round to look at the allotment, but it was a case of looking *for* the allotment. Four perches out of five are one enormous hole and all my potatoes and cabbages have vanished.'

With food supplies growing ever shorter as the war progressed, a few fresh veg could turn an otherwise dull dish into a veritable feast. As such, produce became increasingly valued. An organised barter market sprung up in Croydon, where growers could exchange surplus produce for vouchers to buy clothes and other goods. Elsewhere, there were village raffles offering first prize of a giant onion or some other such delicacy. In innumerable villages and towns, growers armed with shovels and buckets could be seen sprinting down the street after the coalman's cart, hopeful of winning the race for priceless horse manure to spread on their crops. People proudly displayed signs on their garden gates proclaiming, 'This is a Victory Garden.'

Remarkable acts of cooperation became commonplace, from the Gloucestershire village that united to grow potatoes in commercial volumes to the north London dustmen who recycled the waste they collected to feed the pigs they had started to keep. Perhaps most remarkable of all were the residents of Bethnal Green who, pummelled by Nazi air raids, took the land where bombed-out homes and schools once stood and turned it into fertile ground for growing.

Yet more people took on the challenges of animal husbandry for the first time. Rabbit hutches and chicken coops appeared in countless back gardens. Houses were filled with the mysterious aroma attached to the cooking of chicken feed. Others kept beehives to produce their own honey, or joined pig clubs in the hope of feasting upon choice cuts while others had to make do with their minimal bacon rations. On street corners in every major town and city there were 'pig bins' into which citizens were encouraged to deposit their food scraps for porcine sustenance. All this from a nation that, before the war, had looked abroad for its food.

Now among the most fondly remembered of any government initiative in history, the success of the Dig for Victory campaign relied on remarkable feats of organisation, inspired publicity campaigns and a will among the people to undertake whatever they could to 'do their bit'. In an address on the BBC on 27 April 1941, Winston Churchill gave his own typically stirring assessment of the desire on the Home Front to contribute:

Old men, little children, the crippled veterans of former wars, aged women, the ordinary hard-pressed citizen or subject of the

King ... are proud to feel that they stand in the line together with our fighting men, when one of the greatest of causes is being fought out, as fought out it will be, to the end. This is indeed the grand heroic period of our history, and the light of glory shines on all.

On 12 June 1940, an article appeared in the *Manchester Guardian*, headlined 'Half an Acre'. The writer, identified only as 'D.', described the new experience of 'growing your own'. In an understated tone, it speaks of a new way of life and tells a story repeated throughout the country:

Now the potatoes are coming along in eighteen rows, the beetroot is showing strongly, and although the carrots are a mystery and the first two rows of scarlet runners, sown against the weight of local advice, were nipped by a May morning frost the townsmen never heard of, their successors are already running an exciting race with the peas. We are eating our own radishes and spring onions and shortly the infuriating experience of paying four pence for a lettuce will be no more. The celery and the marrows are in. It has all been good fun and good exercise and we are getting proud of it. In fact we now refer to the cottage as The Farm.

Gwen Wild, another contributor to the RHS's documentary on the campaign, recalled fondly:

You'd go home after a Sunday on the allotment and you'd feel really good ... You could go home, sit on the sofa and really relax. Have a nice cup of tea. There is no better feeling in the world ... Dig for Victory was the nub of our existence then. It was our fight. It was the *only* way we could fight.

Yet while we may today look back upon the Dig for Victory campaign as an unprecedentedly successful example of mass mobilisation, there was, in truth, little to suggest such an outcome at the start of the war. Instead, there was a sense that the nation was rather less prepared than it ought to have been. Plans to meet the nation's food requirements had been slow and tentative, and Dig for Victory was started more in hope than in anticipation.

2. A Lesson Not Learned

The Second World War could hardly be said to have come as a surprise, with German Chancellor Adolf Hitler having spent the best part of the 1930s flexing his muscles in the face of international consternation. Yet as conflict had grown inevitable, barely twenty years had passed since the horror of the 'war to end all wars' that cost the lives of a generation. The United Kingdom was stooping beneath the weight of economic meltdown and the prospect of another bloody struggle was a nightmarish spectre for the population at large.

In September 1938, Prime Minister Neville Chamberlain had stood on the tarmac at London's Heston Aerodrome. He was returning from talks with Hitler at the Munich Conference, where Czechoslovakia had been sold down the river in return for a piece of paper that Chamberlain hoped represented 'peace for our time'. It was an episode that brought permanent ignominy down upon him. Winston Churchill reportedly commented: 'England has been offered a choice between war and shame. She has chosen shame, and will get war.' The Munich Agreement, though, encapsulated the dreadful conundrum that the government faced: what do you do in the face of a warmonger when your own people have been all but broken by cataclysmic fighting only a generation before?

Chamberlain's route was soon proved to be misguided and ultimately hopeless. Others, not least Churchill, were sure of that much at the time, and Chamberlain's refusal to heed their warnings has left him open to the withering criticism of hindsight. Yet, to watch footage of his speech at the aerodrome is to witness a leader who could not contemplate another fight, however much cold intellectual analysis suggested it was unavoidable. In this climate, the government of Chamberlain and of Stanley Baldwin before him had only reluctantly made preparations lest they should be drawn once more into military engagement.

For the nation's food situation, this was especially unfortunate. Gearing the nation up to food self-sufficiency was not a project that could be achieved in a matter of weeks or even months. It was a task that demanded years of preparation. Whatever apprehension the prospect of war induced, Westminster and Whitehall were surely obligated to consider how the nation would survive in a worst-case scenario. Nor was there a lack of recent experience upon which to call. A large part of the British population could remember in vivid detail the parlous state of the county's food situation in the 1914–18 War. Yet the government seemed to have learned precious little.

Many of Westminster's big beasts of the time – Churchill and First World War premier David Lloyd George among them – knew first-hand just how perilously close Britain had come to being starved into submission in the latter stages of that conflict. The nation had entered into the war in August 1914 with a widely held belief that fighting would be short and sharp. Few had envisaged the years of debilitating onslaught that lay ahead and, in such an environment, precious little had been done in preparation on the food front, even though home produce then met only around a third of the national requirement. A quarter of a century later and international conflict loomed again, with the UK once more unable to feed herself without relying on foreign imports. The echo through that short span of history was audible yet the authorities seemed caught in stasis. In 1914 and 1915, reasonable harvests and relatively stable food imports had lulled the government into a false sense of security. The Chamberlain government was threatening to adopt a similar position of complacency, neglecting the evidence of damage such a posture might cause.

During the First World War it was only in 1916, when crops failed not only in the United Kingdom but among many of her trade partners too, that there had been a concerted effort to rectify the situation. In December that year, the first Ministry of Food came into being (it would run until 1921) with Lord Devonport as Food Controller, responsible for not only increasing levels of food production but also regulating supply and consumption.

A few months later, a separate Food Production Department was installed at the Board of Agriculture to assist commercial farming operations in obtaining essential equipment, feed, fertilisers and workers. Towards that latter aim, the first version of the Women's Land Army (WLA) was established. At the First World War's end there were over 200,000 women working the land, alongside 30,000 prisoners of war and large numbers of school children as well.

The food situation had become critical from February 1917 when the U-boat blockade of Britain got underway in earnest, with Berlin hoping to starve the United Kingdom out of the war.

In that first month alone, 230 vessels were sunk. More than 1.25 million gross tons of shipping were lost to German submarines between April and June. In food terms, this equated to 52,000 tons of lost fruit and vegetable imports per month, and a further 77,000 tons of other foodstuffs. From 1914 to 1917, something approaching 6 million tons of food disappeared beneath the waves en route to the United Kingdom. At one critical point there were only enough food reserves in the country to see out a further three weeks of fighting.

In a final analysis of how Britain saved herself from impending starvation, there were three main factors involved: first, the adoption of the convoy system from 1917 that, against the expectations of many, neutralised the threat of the German U-boats; second, the introduction, albeit tardily, of rationing in 1918; and third, rapid improvements in the domestic commercial agricultural situation. The latter was somewhat fortuitous, considering the awful yields of 1916, but a vastly improved harvest in 1917 staved off the very real prospect of immediate national disaster. According to the calculations of the agricultural economist, Sir Henry Rew, an additional 2 million acres of permanent pasture and 1.25 million acres of temporary pasture were ploughed up in the United Kingdom between June 1916 and June 1918.

While all might have been lost had the commercial farmers not upped their game, their efforts were consolidated by those of an army of amateur growers. The allotment movement as it was then could trace its origins back to the Allotments Act of 1887, which obliged local councils to provide plots in those areas where there was sufficient demand. Further legislation followed in 1890, 1907 and 1908. By 1914, it is estimated that there were between 450,000 and 600,000 allotment plots available in England alone, leased by a mixture of private landowners, local councils and the church. However, much of the population still regarded allotments in the same manner as their Victorian predecessors had – as a means to occupy the lower classes, keep them from less sociable enterprises, and provide them with a means of bolstering their meagre diets while getting some fresh air away from the stench of their overcrowded neighbourhoods.

Although there was increased uptake of allotments in the early stages of the Great War, it was only as the food crisis worsened – with its accompanying price rises and industrial unrest – that things started to take off. From December 1916, local councils had the legal right to turn over unoccupied land to domestic cultivation. A Cultivation of Land Order the following year empowered them to seize any unused land for the purpose of food production. In addition, there was evidence that the class snobbery regarding allotments was beginning to be challenged. George V made a point of insisting that where there were once picturesque geraniums dotted around the Queen Victoria Memorial close to Buckingham Palace, food crops should be planted instead. It was a strategy taken up by all the Royal Parks.

Meanwhile, the Prime Minister, David Lloyd George was pictured in the press tending veg in the garden of his Walton Heath home; though not, it should be noted, on the greens of his beloved golf club just up the road. With the average man in the street required to hold down his usual job during the week, most allotment tending was done at the weekends, so Randall Davidson, the Archbishop of Canterbury, sanctioned Sunday work for believers. National canteens – a precursor to the British Restaurants of the Second World War – opened and made use of local garden surpluses. Public squares up and down the country, and swathes of land owned by the railway companies, were handed over to eager growers – the railways often earmarking plots exclusively for their employees.

Allotment holding became recognised as a valuable way of contributing to the war effort, and no longer as a mere distraction for the poor. In 1917, there were some 1.5 million plots (a million or so more than in 1914), and by the time of the signing of the armistice in November 1918, it was estimated that there was an allotment for every five households. New allotments since 1916 had provided an extra million tons of food. Rew himself took time to note that the rapid growth in allotment provision contributed significantly to increased vegetable yields.

Overall by 1918, home production had increased by a quarter on 1914 figures, despite the shortages of labour. The men, women and children working away in their gardens or on their plots could take considerable credit for their crucial role in the turnaround in the nation's food fortunes. Lord Ernle, a Conservative politician and renowned agriculturalist, wrote extensively on the experiences of the First World War in the years that followed and keenly expounded the important part that he considered allotments had played in steadying the country's collective nerve.

As a result, in the end it was Germany that buckled first. Somehow Britain kept herself fed and it was Germany that found the cupboard was bare. Raymond A. Cook, writing in 1941 in the gardening guide that he called *Plots against Hitler*, described the situation like this: 'In 1918 the German nation was so short of those foods required to protect them against nervous debility and lassitude that they lost the will to victory

and their sense of national honour, and finally succumbed ...'.
It was a collapse that haunted Adolf Hitler, a scenario he was
determined should play out among the British and not the
Germans come the Second World War. Alas, the lack of
proactive strategy by Britain's pre-war governments only
increased the likelihood.

3. Preparing the Ground

The United Kingdom's immediate post-war drive to put the agricultural industry on a firmer footing resulted in the Agricultural Act of 1920. It made provision for price guarantees across a broad range of staple crops designed to maintain adequate levels of domestic production. It was not a cheap way of going about things though, particularly given that the country was struggling with an economic climate not only drained by the demands of a long conflict but also entering a period of deep uncertainty at home and on the international stage. Politicians of all persuasions were soon espousing a far less protectionist (and expensive) policy, arguing instead for the *laissez-faire* trade environment that had (or so it seemed to those with rose-tinted spectacles) served the nation so well during the glory days of Victoria's reign. Thus the United Kingdom soon returned to its bad habit of massive over-reliance on foreign food imports.

As for the allotment movement, there was precious little effort given to harnessing the momentum garnered over the course of the First World War. What actually transpired was an almost immediate falling off in demand for plots once fighting had ended; this was compounded by compelling calls for land to be given over for more and better housing for returning soldiers and their families. In the ten years from 1918, the number of allotments nationwide fell by about half a million to one million – a disappointing decline despite remaining roughly twice the 1914 levels; and over the course of the 1930s a further 200,000 plots were lost.

By the time Adolf Hitler had become Chancellor of Germany in 1933, the British food production sector was once again moribund. Hitler's rise to power did ring alarm bells though, with Whitehall quickly reaching the conclusion that any conflict would leave the government no choice but to impose a system of food controls, including rationing. Yet it would still take years to put these plans into action. The situation might have been very different had greater heed been given to the urgings of Sir John Boyd Orr for a coherent national food policy.

There had long been a realisation that a great part of the population was not very healthy or robust. When the Second Boer War got underway back in 1899, a recruitment drive had provided ample evidence of the profusion of poor physical specimens among the working classes. In the end, recruiters had no choice but to enforce a height restriction of just 5 foot on potential new soldiers, a reduction of 3 inches on previous limits. The ongoing need to restock the front lines during the First World War had provided yet more anecdotal evidence of the vast numbers of young men from the Home Nations displaying signs of long-term underfeeding and malnutrition. Additionally, the global financial collapse that followed the Wall Street Crash of 1929 led to abject poverty in disparate corners of the United Kingdom. This prompted social campaigners to unite with nutritional scientists, among them Boyd Orr, to paint a clearer picture of just how important diet was for public health.

After seeing active service during the First World War, Boyd Orr, a nutritional physiologist, undertook research work for the Royal Society on the allocation of food resources. In the 1920s, he won fame for his campaigning work to guarantee milk provision for all children. *Food, Health and Income,* arguably his most important publication, appeared in 1936, in which Boyd Orr divided the population of the United Kingdom into six income groups to look at how adequate the diet was in each. His conclusions were shocking – over half of the population lacked the finances to obtain a nutritionally satisfactory diet, with 10 per cent of the population suffering from severe undernourishment. At that time, the Ministry of Agriculture was headed by Walter Elliot, a friend of Boyd Orr and a man firmly of the opinion that the population at large should be encouraged to improve their diets. However, having initially supported Boyd Orr in undertaking the enquiry, he then refused to publish it as an official document, realising that the results were political dynamite and his government was not in a position to vastly improve matters.

Boyd Orr's calls for a coordinated food policy were ignored by consecutive governments who, running a country in the grip of economic depression, were unable or unwilling to confront the problem. Had they not been, the nation might have entered the Second World War with a far better developed system of focused and economical domestic food production. However, his arguments did at least catch the attention of Lord Woolton (to whom Boyd Orr would serve as a trusted advisor during the war when Woolton was Minister of Food). There Boyd Orr's work of the 1930s would at last find an official outlet, guiding

the Ministry's advice on eating healthily and providing a frame-
work for the national rationing system. By then, however, the
government was playing catch-up.

Post-war, Boyd Orr would be invited to serve as the first
Director General of the Food and Agricultural Organization
(1945–8), the international body set up by the Allied nations in
1943 to guide global food policy in the period of post-war
reconstruction. In 1949 Boyd Orr was awarded the Nobel Peace
Prize for his 'great work in the service of mankind which, once
begun, can never be halted'. The fact that his own government
did not make better use of him earlier was undoubtedly an
opportunity missed.

The British government only made the first real steps to address
the potential food problems that a war might throw up in 1935.
Prompted by confirmation of Germany's air force expansion and
Hitler's reintroduction of a mass conscription programme, at the
Ministry of Agriculture, Walter Elliot set up a committee to look
at the issues associated with food production in wartime. In April
1936, the Committee of Imperial Defence also established a sub-
committee to look at wartime food supplies.

The findings of these bodies led to the foundation later that
year of the Food (Defence Plans) Department, which was
nested within the Board of Trade. It was a well-timed innovation
– Italy's invasion of Ethiopia had upped tension among Europe's
powers and increased pressure on the British government to
look more closely at how the country would feed itself in war
(and in particular, how it could guarantee its supplies of wheat).

The new department proved less effective than was hoped,
however. There was a feeling that its hands were tied by its
subordination to the Board of Trade and its work was largely
focused on establishing administrative systems rather than

influencing national policy. Just concerned with food supply, it scarcely gave a nod to the equally important question of food production (which fell under the aegis of the Ministry of Agriculture); the department was also vastly understaffed, an issue that would not be remedied until the 1938 Munich Crisis had suitably concentrated minds.

There was a further problem facing those in favour of stronger government intervention. In certain political lights, this could look very similar to the sort of centralised planning that Joseph Stalin was championing in the Soviet Union and which was anathema to the vast majority of the British voting public. In the event that there was no war, no major party in British politics wanted to face accusations of championing a communist-style collectivisation programme. The reluctance of government to get stuck in was, therefore, to some extent understandable but damagingly unhelpful. Essentially, government food policy was toothless. The reality was that in the event of war, the authorities would have to be vastly more hands-on than pre-war preparations suggested.

In July 1937, there was evidence that the government was finally beginning to treat the food question with the urgency it deserved. The decision was taken to prepare and print ration books for everyone in the country, and to put them into storage until they might be required. In the event, printing was only completed a few weeks before war was declared but, even so, the intention was good.

In terms of production, the immediate pre-war focus quite rightly fell on the commercial agricultural sector, with little thought yet given to how amateur growers might contribute. The Ministry of Agriculture encouraged farmers to turn their attentions to vegetable and cereal crops, which offered greater nutritional value to more people per acre of land than meat. Where one acre of grazing pasture could support enough animals to provide meat for one or maybe two people, the same area could produce enough wheat to satisfy twenty bellies or enough potatoes for forty. In addition, cows, sheep, pigs and poultry all consumed cereal crops at a rate wholly unsustainable at a time of national crisis. Of course, the Ministry was keen to preserve enough animal farming to meet the nation's basic needs, but the advent of war marked a sea change in British agriculture away from livestock towards crops.

Plans were prepared for a 'ploughing-up' campaign, under the terms of which farmers received payments of £1 for each acre of grassland ploughed up in 1938, rising to a giddy £2 in 1939. In many cases, ground was prepared for cropping for the first time in centuries. The aim was to put roughly 2 million acres of idle land into production by the 1940 harvest. There were further subsidies available to help with land drainage and to buy essential equipment and supplies. Meanwhile, farmers and farm labourers over the age of twenty-one were to be granted reserved status, exempting them from call-ups to the armed services.

In 1938, the Essential Commodities (Reserves) Act paved the way for the government to buy and stockpile key goods. The Chancellor's budget speech in April 1938 laid out plans, for instance, for the purchase of supplies of wheat and sugar large enough to last out at least the first few months of a war. Whitehall worked closely with private sector trade associations in an attempt to regulate both production and demand of virtually all major foodstuffs, and to supervise food imports. Practically every major crop and imported food stuff came under the purview of a dedicated control board.

The 1939 Emergency Powers (Defence) Act strengthened the government's hand, giving the Ministry of Agriculture greater control over food production and allowing it to take over farms if land was not being used in a satisfactory manner. That summer, sufficient food was set aside for basic 'iron rations' in the event of mass evacuations from cities under threat of aerial bombing. In addition, an Acquisition of Food (Excessive Quantities) Order of 31 August 1939 curbed stockpiling by individuals, sensibly prohibiting anyone from buying in excess of a single week's worth of supplies.

The Cultivation of Land (Allotments) Order of 1939 finally gave a clue to the government's intentions regarding allotment plots and their role in the food production drive. Local councils were awarded the power to requisition unoccupied land, parks and playing fields and convert them into allotments. They could also grant permission to keep livestock on plots, while allotment trespass became a statutory offence, indicating that the wartime amateur grower was to be treated with respect. Veg growing, one could surmise, was to be regarded as more than simply a frivolous hobby.

Such was the story of how the plans to deal with the food shortages that war would bring were put into place. It was a narrative regularly coloured by half-heartedness and incoherence in government. Numerous committees were established, reports commissioned and orders enacted, but at times progress was painfully slow, with short-term concerns of the market prioritised above all else for too long. It was, perhaps, indicative of a desperate hope on the part of those implementing these plans that peace would somehow triumph before their provisions need truly be tested. By the time there was consensus that there would be no such reprieve, the nation was on the back foot.

4. War Arrives

At 11:45 on the morning of 3 September 1939, Prime Minister Neville Chamberlain broadcast to the nation, delivering the news no one wanted to hear: 'This morning the British Ambassador in Berlin handed the German Government a final note stating that unless we heard from them by 11.00 a.m. that they were prepared at once to withdraw their troops from Poland, a state of war would exist between us. I have to tell you that no such undertaking has been received, and that consequently this country is at war with Germany.'

In her diary entry for 6 September that year, Joan Strange provided her own glimpse of the national mood:

> … life has suddenly become very difficult under wartime conditions. Very few people felt this terrible blow would fall and right up to Sunday morning (3 September) there was a glimmer of hope. On Friday the Germans 'crossed the frontiers to resist the Poles' and the newspapers immediately declared 'war begins'. Everyone's spirits sank but rose again when Mr Chamberlain gave Hitler one more chance in a message sent on Saturday with a time limit up at eleven o'clock on Sunday

morning. In the meantime the 'blackouts' have started, no one must show a glimmer of light anywhere ... Some food especially sugar is very scarce ...

If the public had been caught on the hop as Joan suggests, the government was not much better off. With regard to food, the UK's great Achilles' heel remained its over-reliance on imports. In 1939, some 55 million tons of food, equivalent to three-quarters of the national total, came from overseas. That encompassed 51 per cent of all meat, 70 per cent of cheese, 73 per cent of sugar, 80 per cent of fruit and 90 per cent of cereals. Spain and France jointly supplied some 90 per cent of Britain's onions, a staple of British cuisine that could so easily have been produced on UK soil. If the First World War food situation had taught the government and their advisors anything, it was that believing adequate trade inflows could be maintained was folly. Not only was it impossible to know if shipping convoys could be protected as efficiently as they had been at the end of the Great War, it also ignored the fact that those ships would be needed to transport other essential supplies and personnel.

The government had laid out plans to survive a war lasting three years. It was, perhaps, not an unreasonable timetable at that stage, and it is arguable as to whether anyone could have made sensible predictions for a timescale extending much beyond it. But as we now know, it was a significant underestimation of the six years of war that actually transpired, and the United Kingdom entered into conflict with a mere four months' worth of stockpiled supplies. The Minister for Agriculture and Fisheries, Reginald Dorman-Smith, explained to farmers that, in partnership with the government, it was their job 'to increase, in an orderly fashion, our home production of essential foodstuffs

— a task just as vital to the nation as that which has to be carried out by the armed forces'.

The position of the amateur grower was less clear. The home production campaign of the First World War was not sufficiently structured nor had detailed records been kept to be able to give anything like a comprehensive picture of what a similar scheme might achieve in this new war. The hope was that, if implemented earlier, more energetically and more efficiently than two decades previously, it might prove a valuable means of keeping the larder stocked. Dorman-Smith appeared on the BBC on 3 October 1939, a month after Chamberlain had made his grim announcement to the British people, to formally introduce what was to become known as the Dig for Victory campaign, but which was at that stage called Grow More Food:

> It is clearly our duty, just as it is a matter of elementary wisdom, to try to make doubly and trebly sure that we will fight and win this war on full stomachs. To do this we want not only the big man with the plough but also the little man with the spade to get busy this autumn. We are launching a nationwide campaign to obtain recruits to the ranks of the food producers. Half a million more allotments properly worked will provide potatoes and vegetables that will feed another million adults and one and a half million children for eight months of the year. The matter is not one that can wait. So let's get going. Let 'Dig for Victory' be the motto of everyone with a garden and of every able-bodied man and woman capable of digging an allotment in their spare time.

The basic aims of the initial phase of the campaign were deceptively simple: to encourage as many men, women and children as possible to use their back gardens or apply to local authorities for an allotment plot (typically covering an area of 10 rods, or 30 by 90 feet) to supply their families (and perhaps a few friends) with enough vegetables to see them through the big part of the year.

But the challenge of administering a campaign as broad-ranging and complex as Dig for Victory was a Herculean one. It was not a case of simply handing round a few forks and spades to willing gardeners and waiting for them to stock the national larder. Instead the government needed to identify exactly what crops to concentrate on in order to save shipping, relieve the commercial agricultural industry and compensate for potential deficiencies in Britain's nutritional needs. Then it had to provide suitable land for those without their own gardens to work on, match it to appropriate applicants, and establish local infra-structures to oversee the efficient running of plots, and to provide essential supplies and equipment as well as advice and support. Finally, systems had to be put in place to ensure that the fruits (and veg) of the campaign were put to good use. All of this required not only an adept bureaucracy but a public relations campaign that would educate and capture the imagination of millions who had never previously considered themselves as possessors of green fingers.

As Dorman-Smith's original announcement would suggest, the campaign was the baby of the Ministry of Agriculture. However, elements of Dig for Victory necessarily fell under the jurisdiction of other departments with whom the Ministry of Agriculture needed to establish clear boundaries of respon-sibility. Though the ministries of Education and Health would sporadically have an interest in its execution over the ensuing years, this principally meant the Ministry of Food. Swinging into life on 8 September 1939, this new ministry had been primed for action in the months prior to the war after emerging out of the Food (Defence Plans) Department. William Morrison was at the helm, charged with the job of running food procurement, distribution and rationing. In simplistic terms, he was responsible for making sure food was shared out equitably.

The two men at the head of these crucially important departments when the war commenced seemed ideally suited to their roles and promised much. Dorman-Smith had been born in County Cavan, Ireland in 1899 into a family with a rich farming heritage. By the age of just thirty-two he was Vice President of the National Farmers' Union, and three years later had secured himself a seat in parliament as the Conservative MP for Petersfield. In 1936 he was named President of the National Farmers' Union, and when Neville Chamberlain appointed him Minister of Agriculture in January 1939, few disputed that he was the obvious choice.

William Morrison was, meanwhile, put in charge at the Ministry of Food, having previously ruled the roost at the Ministry of Agriculture from October 1936 until Dorman-Smith replaced him. Morrison had served with honour as a captain during the First World War and had received the Military Cross. A much-loved figure within the Conservative party, known for his imposing stature and silky oratorical skills delivered in a mellifluous Scottish accent, the immediate pre-war years had proved somewhat difficult for him. Though a critic of appeasement, his refusal to resign in the wake of the Munich debacle weakened him in the eyes of many. Furthermore, his belief that war was not a complete inevitability left him hamstrung during his stint at the Ministry of Agriculture, as he refused to oversee a radical (and, retrospectively, much-needed) programme of war preparation for fear of damaging the industry in the case of ongoing peace. Nonetheless, it was hoped that his background at Agriculture would serve him well in the newly created Food Ministry.

Certainly, Dorman-Smith was quick to introduce the necessary administrative structures to get the Dig for Victory campaign or, more accurately, the Grow More Food campaign, up and running. The British agricultural sector was put on to a formal war footing on 1 September 1939, two days before Chamberlain's declaration of war. On 3 September itself, the County War Agricultural Executive Committees began operating under orders received in telegrams directly from Dorman-Smith. Initially, there were forty-eight English and twelve Welsh CWAECs (or War Ags as they were popularly known) and they were to play an instrumental role in the coming years as a conduit for information exchange between central government and growers, both amateur and professional. Importantly, they also had the power to dispossess owners of any farms that were deemed to be uncooperative or inefficient.

The composition of the committees had been decided before the war, and usually consisted of between eight to twelve representatives who were *au fait* with the particular agricultural conditions of their local areas and were prepared to work unpaid to ensure the maximum productivity of the land. Each committee was headed by a chairman, supported by an executive officer and a secretary. Most members were farmers and nurserymen but there tended to be at least one landowner too, as well as representatives of farm workers and, often, the Women's Land Army (WLA).

The War Ags were then subdivided into sub-committees to look at specific agricultural questions and district committees to ensure full geographical coverage. A member of a District Committee might typically cover an area of 5,000 acres and was expected to maintain channels of communication with all the farmers and growers within that area. Latterly, some district committees worked on a system of one representative for every parish.

The principal role of the committees was to make growers aware of what the government needed in order to feed the nation while also keeping central government informed of what was happening on the ground. In addition, the War Ags were responsible for administering various grants and credit schemes, ensuring supplies of equipment, fertiliser and seeds and, in some cases, identifying and preparing derelict land for cultivation. They were also expected to provide expert advice, and to this end employed paid technical officers, who perhaps unsurprisingly tended to be more concerned with the needs of professional farmers than keen gardeners and allotment growers.

As might be imagined, being the bearer of sometimes unpopular tidings from central government did not always make for an easy relationship between growers and the War Ags. The image of War Ag. members as bossy, autocratic and occasionally draconian was a popular one, and from June 1940 the Ministry appointed twelve liaison officers, responsible for around five CWAECs each, to try to improve the flow of information. By the end of the war these wholly voluntary War Ags had dealt with almost 2,000 circulars from Dorman-Smith and his successors.

While the role of the keen amateur might not have been

their prime concern, the committees also oversaw the activities of County Horticultural Advisers who were charged with helping any gardening societies and organisations that requested assistance. They also worked closely with Land Commissioners from the Ministry on how best to execute the legal powers delegated to them by the Minister, just as when, for example, Dorman-Smith sent a circular to each local council on 18 September 1939 authorising additional land to be let for allotments.

The debate over whether to sacrifice playing fields to production proved particularly heated. In the early days of the drive, local councils were largely happy to yield to pressure to give up what were (so the thinking went) mere leisure facilities secondary to the cause of producing essential food stocks. However, the arguments in favour of retaining recreational areas were subtle but potent. A correspondent in *The Times* took on the subject in March 1940:

> Land now being converted into allotments forms in many cases the 'lungs' of a city, providing for town-dwellers a valuable open space for recreation and exercise, and fears have been expressed that the creation of allotments may have encroached unduly on the public and private recreation facilities. As the President of the MCC pointed out in a letter published in *The Times* yesterday, a sufficient area for the conduct of open-air sport is necessary to the welfare of the nation.

In an address to the National Playing Fields Association in May 1940, Lord Cavan also outlined his concerns for the long-term situation:

... there is evidence that too many local authorities are disposed to yield to pressure and find allotment space by sacrificing playing fields. Such grounds are of vital importance for maintaining public health and morale and as recreation grounds for troops under training, and the eventual cost of restoring them for play would involve serious outlay.

A.B. Clements, editor of the *Sporting Life*, was rather more abrupt:

The virtuous wrath ... against the continuance of some forms of sport in wartime is misplaced ... There is an enormous number of people in our industrial areas who cannot dig for victory, for they have no plot ... For mental relief from the drudgery of the factory they should, no doubt, read the classics, but we have to face up to the fact that some quite good workers are not intellectually equipped for such diversion ... I contend that so long as sports meetings do not hinder the war effort their effect on morale is ample justification for continuance.

Involvement in such debates was inevitable for members of the War Ags and most realised that their largely thankless position was unlikely to win them new friends. But Neville Chamberlain was clear about the value of their work when he addressed a meeting of all the county chairmen in February 1940: '... in the opinion of the government the issue of this war depends just as much upon what we can do to produce more food at home as it does upon the more conspicuous exploits of our fighting men on the seas or in the air or on the land'.

Local councils also played a crucial role. They established

Home Produce Councils and Horticultural Committees in large numbers to look into the matter of food production, with local Parks' Superintendents normally their focal point. These bodies were key in identifying and preparing land that might be suitable for allotments, not to mention processing applications for plots from the public, setting up demonstration plots, and providing advice and support to often novice gardeners. With the average local authority allotment measuring 30 feet by 90 feet and rents averaging between 3s. and 10s. per annum, 'growing your own' became a viable option for vast swathes of the population who could never previously have considered it. Meanwhile, Village Produce Associations were vital in offering additional encouragement, regularly arranging talks or slide shows and promoting the messages of the Ministry of Agriculture.

By and large, growers took well to such efforts. Dorothy Hinchcliffe, a Ministry of Agriculture inspector in Westmorland and North Lancashire, remembered that in general people were responsive to the help on offer and impressively proactive: 'People knew the urgency of it. They did it really of their own accord ... I'd go round saying are you doing so and so and I'd generally find they were well ahead of me.'

Yet not everyone warmed to unsought help, particularly if they deemed they were being patronised by individuals who knew less than they did. Take this account by Eric Hobbis, a popular gardener of the time who went on to broadcast for the BBC. He was a major figure in the Dig for Victory campaign around Bristol, where there were demonstration allotment plots in half-a-dozen districts, and was often to be found travelling around the area on advisory visits. For a relative newcomer to the region, these trips could prove tricky on occasion, especially when local signage had been removed for defence reasons. On one journey Eric asked a local farm hand if the road he was on was the correct one for a particular farm. 'I dunno,' came the reply. 'Does the path across the field go to such-and-such farm?' 'I dunno.' 'Does this road go to such-and-such village?' 'I dunno.' Exasperated, Eric retorted, 'You don't know much, do you?' The farm hand replied, 'Enough. I bain't lost and you be.'

Another gardener, a Mr W.H.J. Fox from Dorchester, struggled to think warmly of the County Hall advisers sent to check that every inch of available land was being wisely used. 'They had been hurriedly trained,' he recalled, 'had never used a spade or a pair of secateurs and were thoroughly unpractical ... They knew almost nothing about the land and its seasons.'

Then there was the Ministry of Information, which was the primary organ for spreading the word about the Dig for Victory campaign but which had made a most inauspicious start. On 4 September 1939, the day after war was declared, the Ministry of Information began its operations, producing and distributing publicity and propaganda on behalf of other central government bodies. The British people are historically averse to the idea of its governments filtering and tweaking the information they receive, so such an institution had few forerunners, although there had been a Department of Information and then a Ministry of Information formed in the latter stages of the Great War.

However, the public could hardly be said to have taken those government mouthpieces to their hearts. Rather, the people emerged from the carnage of that war devastated by unprecedented loss and feeling utterly misled by their national leaders. Let it be remembered, the First World War was supposed to have been a little bit of trouble on the continent, with the boys sure to be home by Christmas 1914. No one had expected that four years later there would be almost a million dead (over 2 per cent of the total population) and 1.7 million wounded. The First World War represented a watershed in British history in terms of social ordering. Stung by a sense of betrayal, it was the point at which the masses who had previously maintained a significant level of deference to their supposed social superiors concluded that it was dangerous to believe anything their 'betters' told them. This produced an unenviable climate in which to introduce a new propaganda ministry just over two decades later.

While the new Ministry of Information was not activated until the Second World War started, it had been planned by the Committee of Imperial Defence since autumn 1935. Its subsequent four years of evolution occurred in some secrecy, the government believing, no doubt correctly, that should the activities of this department become public knowledge, it would be taken as a sign of the inevitability of conflict. The team responsible for drawing up plans for the Ministry of Information was made up mostly of volunteer experts from within government, other public institutions and private media organisations. A semi-official 'shadow' Ministry was instituted in 1936, with Stephen Tallents (then head of public relations at the BBC) as its director, until he was sacked in January 1939 in a dispute over how it should be structured and staffed.

Born in London in 1884, Tallents was a talented career civil servant who had gained a reputation in the post-First World War years as an expert in public relations, notably at the Empire Marketing Board. Indeed, it has been claimed that the phrase 'public relations' originated from him. In the early 1930s, he headed up the publicity section of the General Post Office, where he developed the renowned GPO Film Unit (which as the Crown Film Unit would produce some of the most famous films of the Second World War). In 1935, Tallents moved to the BBC and subsequently headed up the BBC's Overseas Service but fell victim to internal politics and was forced out in September 1941. Bewilderingly, his skills were allowed to go to waste for the remainder of the war. Only afterwards was he given due recognition as a pioneer of public relations, serving as the inaugural President of the Institute of Public Relations in 1948–9 and again in 1952–3.

Even with Stephen Tallents' skills, the sailing was not always smooth at the shadow Ministry, with many government departments unwilling to cede control to a centralised department as they already had their own public relations sections. There was a general acceptance, though, that propaganda was likely to play a crucial role in any upcoming war. Hitler had already shown himself a master manipulator of information in his own domestic rise to power. Meanwhile, the United Kingdom, still reeling from the last war and from economic depression, was hardly at the height of her confidence. It was clear the government would need to be sensitive to this vulnerability and take extreme care in how it communicated with the people.

It is thus somewhat surprising that the Ministry in its early months was so utterly chaotic and ineffective. After Tallents, the Ministry came under the stewardship of Hugh Macmillan. A Scotsman already in his late sixties, he was a judge who had served as Lord Advocate in the Labour government of Ramsay MacDonald in the 1920s and was cursed with a propensity to rub people up the wrong way. Heading the Ministry of Information until January 1940, Macmillan's job was made no easier by the fact that his tenure coincided with the height of the 'Phoney War' (a term that broadly covers the period from the declaration of war in September 1939 until May 1940), during which time the government was unwilling to share much at all with the gentlemen of the press. Fleet Street had an in-built resistance anyway to being told what they should be reporting, and were riled by what they perceived as the avalanche of patronising platitudes gushing forth from officials in place of hard information. As the Ministry's Parliamentary Secretary Harold Nicolson wrote in 1941, it was 'the most unpopular department in the whole British Commonwealth of nations'.

After a short tenure, Macmillan gave way to John Reith who, as Director-General of the BBC, had once been Tallents' boss. Another Scot, Reith was a physically imposing figure, measuring 6 foot 6 inches in height, and had his own reputation for being difficult to work with. But his track record as the man who had moulded the BBC was a remarkable one, and he was a logical choice for the ministerial post. Having left the BBC in 1938 for a somewhat unsatisfying spell heading up Imperial Airways, he was keen for a new job to get his teeth into.

Alas, even with such promising credentials, Reith did not vastly improve the Ministry's functioning. Nor was the job of promoting food production made any easier by having to work with the distinctly lacklustre and uninspiring 'Grow More Food' official branding. The first 'Grow More Food' bulletin was published in October 1939, having prepared in cooperation with the Royal Horticultural Society. Entitled 'Grow for Winter as well as Summer', in many ways it was an admirable little pamphlet that served as the manifesto for the campaign. Its cheerful front page read:

Vegetables for you and your family every week of the year. Never a week without food from your garden or allotment. Not only fresh peas and lettuce in June, new potatoes in July, but all the health-giving vegetables in Winter, when supplies are scarce ... Savoys, Sprouts, Kale, Sprouting Broccoli, Onions, Leeks, Carrots, Parsnips and Beet. Vegetables all the year round if you DIG WELL AND CROP WISELY.

Attached was a colourful fold-out cropping plan, which suggested dividing your vegetable patch into three sections, each sown with one of three categories of crop: miscellaneous crops, such as peas, beans and onions; potatoes and root crops; and winter and spring green crops. This was to be done every year over a three year cycle. It was altogether a sensible and well thought out scheme (crop rotation 'is the only sound basis for vegetable growing', claimed the Ministry). However, an unfortunate misprint, substituting feet for inches, resulted in some less-than-helpful planting instructions for marrows. A certain section of the readership was left aghast and immediately took up attitudes against the campaign as a whole, ranging from gentle scepticism to outright sneering.

In addition, there were some fairly spectacular administrative blunders that tested the patience of the public and left the nascent campaign open to ridicule. Take, for instance, a letter published in *The Times* in December 1939 from a Graham Reid. He wrote:

Sir, – My father, aged eighty-one and confined to his room the past two years, has also been picked out by the Ministry of Agriculture as a fit person to be exhorted to 'Dig for Victory'. His garden is about one-eighth of an acre. The packet delivered by post "On His Majesty's Service" contained ninety-four leaflets together with a typed slip informing him where further supplies may be obtained.

This was hardly the image of unwasteful thriftiness that the Ministry was trying to promote. And neither was this an isolated incident. Another correspondent, C. W. Cecil Baker, wrote a few days later that her ninety-year-old and virtually blind grandmother had been 'exhorted by our amazingly enterprising Ministry of Agriculture to "Dig for Victory." She, too, received the enormous package of nearly a hundred leaflets. Fortunately the good old lady retains her keen sense of humour.' At the end of February 1940, even the Home Publicity Department of the Ministry of Information had the good grace to admit that these early mail-outs had not gone quite as well as might have been hoped: '... the "Dig for Victory" pamphlets fell into strange hands – the hands of invalid societies, hospital almoners and keepers of goats.'

In a parliamentary debate on 6 February 1940, David Lloyd George (Prime Minister during the previous World War but by 1940 in his late seventies and holding only the more modest position of MP for Caernarvon Boroughs), launched a rather more serious attack on the execution of the campaign, which he believed was being held back by central government meanness:

> Then we have to get all the gardeners in the country. There is a great scheme. An appeal is made, through all sorts of institutions, to stir up their energies. The Government say, 'We will provide fertilisers.' But the Treasury, in a Memorandum, say that it must not cost more than £1,000. That is real profligacy ... it is a case

of a snip here, a snip there ... You cannot dig for victory with a pair of Treasury scissors.

The Ministries of both Food and Agriculture thus spent the early months of the war to some extent chasing their tails. With their focus necessarily on commercial food production, 'Grow More Food' was left to coast along.

5. Foot and Mouthpiece

In order to gain momentum, it was crucial that the Grow More Food campaign got the media onside. Ostensibly, this should not have posed too great a challenge, for what was there to object to? Here was an opportunity to foster camaraderie and give a sense of purpose to those who might otherwise have felt left out of the war effort. Growers got to spend time in the open air, often surrounded by loved ones and close friends, carrying out labours that kept them fit and which produced satisfyingly tangible results – and all in the interests of having more and better to eat.

Sure enough, the papers started to report on the campaign in generally favourable terms, with only the occasional glitch. For instance, the *National Garden Club Magazine*, which began publication in the spring of 1940, was given a slap on the wrist for its slogan 'Dig to Eat', which was considered too downbeat by the powers that be. In the early months of the war, Reginald Dorman-Smith's pronouncements were, in general, dutifully reproduced in print while column inches were willingly given over to particularly heart-warming or newsworthy titbits born of the campaign.

The problem, though, was that while no one doubted the worthy intentions of 'Grow More Food', worthiness alone does not sell papers or stir spirits. Nor did the campaign stand much chance of wrestling off the front page tales of military entanglements on the continent or the latest twists and turns in international relations. Going through the newspaper archives now, it is striking how long the press could go without reporting at all on the campaign. There was simply too much else of more immediate import with which to fill their pages (the number of which were themselves reduced due to wartime constraints).

Nor could journalists rely on the relevant government departments to provide them with particularly sparky copy. Dorman-Smith's foreword to *Grow More Food Bulletin No. 1* was symptomatic of the problem; the task of growing more food sounded like it was all rather hard work:

> In war we must make every effort. All the potatoes, all the cabbages and all the other vegetables we can produce will be needed. That is why I appeal to you, lovers of this great country of ours, to dig, to cultivate, to sow and to plant.
>
> Our fellow countrymen in the Forces abroad and at home are playing their part. I am confident that you equally will do yours by producing the maximum food from gardens and allotments.

In the end it fell to Fleet Street, always attuned to a catchy sound bite, to prompt the crucial rebranding of 'Grow More Food' as 'Dig for Victory'. Back then, Dig for Victory was the phrase that captured the public's attention, driving the campaign on to greater heights. Today, it is redolent with so much of what the popular memory associates with the British people and 'their finest hour'. Somewhat surprisingly, credit for coining perhaps the most enduring of all wartime slogans should almost certainly rest with a young Michael Foot.

Foot is remembered now for his long-standing relationship with the Labour Party, during which he led it to virtual capitulation against Margaret Thatcher's Conservatives in the 1983 general election. In 1939, he was the fiery left-wing leader writer for the London *Evening Standard*. The paper's original call to horticultural arms was printed in the edition of 6 September 1939, under the bold headline 'DIG'. It posed a rousing challenge to those on the Home Front, forging an association between seemingly run-of-the-mill domestic labour and the defeat of the abhorred enemy. With the Ministry of Agriculture at that stage dithering over the introduction of rationing and Dorman-Smith a month away from his appeal for new recruits on the 'Garden Front', it was the first concerted attempt to use rhetoric to stir the nation's army of diggers:

Britain must learn to dig ... Not only must we dig in the cities. Every spare half acre from the Shetlands to the Scillies must feel the shear of the spade ... Turn up each square foot of turf. Root out bulbs and plant potatoes. Spend your Sunday afternoon with a hoe instead of in the hammock. Take a last look at your tennis lawn and then hand it over to the gardener. And if you meet any poor fool attempting to beat the plough share into a sword, tell him that this war may be won in the farms as well as on the battlefield ... More food from our own fields can thwart the Nazi raiders who will search for our food ships beneath the seas. Remember, therefore, that food wins victories as surely as gunpowder ... By husbanding our food resources, by searching out new soil from which to add to our stores, we may contribute perhaps decisively to the finish of this contest. Tell your neighbour and remember yourself that the order is to dig. The spade may prove as mighty as the sword. DIG.

However, it would be a further six days (on 12 September 1939) before the *Standard* finally used the famous phrase:

The Germans remember 1918. Hence their U-boat campaign, by which they have sunk some 70,000 tons of British shipping in the first week of war. The figure is not alarming, for in April 1917 the weekly toll averaged more than 100,000 tons. Our Navy will smite back and reduce the total, just as it did in that earlier contest. But the submarine can be defeated on every square foot of British soil as well as on the high seas. So the order which the *Evening Standard* gave a week ago must be rammed home: Dig for Victory.

Both editorials were printed without bylines, but the obituary of Michael Foot that appeared in the *Independent* newspaper on 4 March 2010 seems to confirm him as the man responsible. By a quirk of the obituary writer's profession, the piece commemorating Foot was written by Lord Ardwick, who himself had died in 1994. Presumably the article had been tucked away in a filing cabinet in the intervening years waiting for Foot, as it were, to kick the bucket. Lord Ardwick, a much-respected lifelong newspaper man himself, described how in the spring of 1940, when he was plain old John Beavan, he had joined the staff of the *Standard*. He was introduced to the 27-year-old Foot by the editor Frank Owen (Foot was to succeed Owen in that role in 1942), who told Beavan that 'Michael's a Stalinite.' We may only muse as to whether Foot at some level saw Dig for Victory as an opportunity to promote the return of the land to the masses. Whatever the motivation, Beavan recalled in an aside that 'Once, Foot beseeched the readers to dig their vegetable plots, dig them wide and "dig for victory", thus providing one of the Second World War's best-remembered slogans.'

We might also ponder whether, without Foot's flash of inspiration, we would remember quite so fondly the more prosaic 'Grow More Food' campaign. Despite officialdom lagging some months behind, within weeks of Dorman-Smith's official announcement of the campaign, the world at large was talking in terms of 'Dig for Victory'. Though Foot appears to be receiving the credit for his bit of brilliance only in death, it should surely rate highly among the long list of his life's achievements.

The wireless was of equal importance to Fleet Street in communicating the message at this stage of the campaign, and it was at the BBC that the campaign's greatest popular figure worked. Now largely forgotten, his name was Cecil Henry (C.H.) Middleton, but he was known affectionately by all simply as Mr Middleton. At the campaign's outset, when neither energy nor exposure levels were yet up to speed, he was its single most important promoter. In his role as the BBC's hugely popular chief gardening broadcaster, Middleton's gentle manner and homely advice made him the perfect character to guide the new army of domestic vegetable growers and allotment holders.

Mr Middleton was born on 22 February 1886 in the tiny hamlet of Weston by Weedon in the south-west of Northamptonshire. A love of gardening was bred into him – his father, John, was

employed in the gardens of Weston Hall by Sir George Sitwell
(a nobleman whose achievements included the invention of a
pistol for shooting wasps, those eternal foes of the gardener!).
Young Cecil spent a good deal of his time keeping his father
company and in so doing came to know well the three Sitwell
children, Edith, Osbert and Sacheverell.

In his teenage years, Middleton assisted his father in a
professional capacity and at the age of seventeen took up a
position with a seed company in London. Keen to expand his
knowledge, he spent his free time in private study and eventually secured a position as a student gardener at the Botanical
Gardens in Kew. At the onset of the First World War, he found
employment in the Horticultural Division of the Board of
Agriculture, working in its food production section. He
subsequently passed the exams for the National Diploma in
Horticulture and went to work as a horticultural instructor at
Surrey County Council.

It was in this latter role that he came to the attention of the
BBC, which had been experimenting with several gardening
formats since its emergence in 1922. It had used a number of
notable speakers, including the novelist Marion Cran and the
aristocratic garden-lover Vita Sackville-West, whose passionate
nature, we now know, was rather more evident in her personal
life than in her career on the wireless. There were also short
informative programmes made in partnership with the Royal
Horticultural Society but, in common with much of the BBC's
early output, the pieces tended to be disconcertingly formal. It
was hoped that Mr Middleton, bespectacled and neatly
presented, might adopt a slightly more relaxed approach while
still maintaining the corporation's high standards. He made his
debut over the airwaves on 9 May 1931. His first utterance,

informal and amiable, set the tone that marked out the rest of his broadcasting career: 'Good afternoon. Well, it's not much of a day for gardening, is it?'

In September 1934, Middleton got his own Friday evening show, *In the Garden*. In time, it would be renamed *In Your Garden* and its broadcast slot moved to Sunday afternoons, transmitting all year round except for a few weeks' break during the summer. With an audience that reached 3.5 million, he was one of the BBC's biggest draws. His secret was an ability to make each listener feel that they were being personally addressed by a man who treated them as his equal. In 1937, from a specially created plot at Alexandra Palace, he made the first gardening broadcast on British television.

Never forgetting his roots despite his success, Middleton was always on the side of the 'little gardener'. In a 1935 broadcast, he rallied against the image of amateur horticulturalists as 'funny old men with battered hats and old moth-eaten trousers and with whiskers and very little intelligence'. 'Generally speaking,' he said, 'they're very much as other men are – perhaps a little better in many ways: wholesome, decent-living people who love their work – usually straight and often deeply religious people, perhaps without knowing it, and certainly without shouting about it. They work hand in hand with Nature and they know that their work is under the direct supervision of the Great Architect.'

The idea of patronising his listeners was odious to him. One critic, Wilfrid Rooke Ley, appraised his talents in the *Catholic Herald* of 27 September 1935 like this:

It is the art of Mr Middleton to address himself to the lowest common denominator of horticultural intelligence without the faintest hint of superiority or condescension. He will assume that your soil is poor, and your pocket poor. All he asks is that your hopes are high and your Saturday afternoons at his service … he has the prettiest humour. He stands for common sense and has the gift of consolation.

There can scarcely have been a man alive better suited to making the best out of difficult horticultural circumstances. Another critic of the day, Peter Black, wrote of how Middleton 'seemed to enlarge the business of cultivating one's garden into a serene and comforting philosophy'. In 2008, Byron Rogers described him as 'the first English national working-class hero, apart from footballers and hangmen'.

With the coming of the war, the Ministry of Agriculture wrote to the BBC, seeking an assurance that *In Your Garden* would not be axed. The BBC, never keen to over-praise its talent, considered the question and in March 1940 concluded:

> … his talks are inherently better value than any alternatives that could be found. From the point of view of propaganda or practical advice it is unlikely that we could find speakers who could rise above his level. On the other hand, they might easily fall below it and would not be likely ever to rise to the heights to which he can aspire on occasions.

Nonetheless, in early 1940 there were parties within the Ministry of Agriculture who moved to cut Middleton out of the campaign, only to be forced to keep him on when presented with evidence of his enormous appeal. Later in the year he delivered a reading at a special service conducted at St Martin-in-the-Fields in Trafalgar Square for the blessing of allotments.

Dig for Victory had not found its way directly to the heart of Home Front life, but from the unpromising seeds of the Grow More Food campaign, it now at least had a killer slogan and a broadcasting patron with the skills and reach to build momentum.

6. Breaking the Ground

As late as August 1940, *The Times* noted of Dig for Victory that, 'Its results so far have been patchy …', but there were other, more fundamental reasons for the campaign's slow pace in the early phase of the war than merely a lack of media exposure.

Firstly, the full seriousness of the United Kingdom's food situation took some time to filter through to the population at large. The implementation of rationing had been delayed until 6 January 1940 due to the fervency of the opposition it engendered, especially from the press. The *Daily Express*, for instance, wrote in November 1939 that: 'The public should revolt against the food rationing system, that dreadful and terrible iniquity … There is no necessity for the trouble and expense of rationing.' Such attitudes clearly unnerved the government, with William Morrison at the Ministry of Food having announced to the press on 8 September 1939 that 'There are splendid stocks of food in the country,' and 'There is no need to fear any shortage.' It must have been a claim he knew was, at the very least, questionable. In terms of Digging for Victory, potential growers were left scratching their heads as to why they should bother.

This was also the stage of the Phoney War. It was something of a misnomer, given that the British Navy was actually involved in several bloody encounters during the period, while Luftwaffe raids over Britain began in October 1939 with an attack on the Forth Bridge. However, major military engagements of note were few and far between until the Norwegian Campaign in April 1940. So, while the nation's fighting forces went on in something of a state of limbo, British civilians adapted to a curious new existence in which they were subject to rationing, shortages and blackouts. They also endured the social upheaval attendant with mass evacuations and consumed a succession of depressing stories of continental Europe crumbling in the face of German advance. Getting used to this situation took time, and ordinary people were still unsure how badly the war would affect them and for how long. In such circumstances, it is little surprise that for many the undertaking of food production was low on the list of immediate priorities.

Furthermore, some of those best equipped to Dig for Victory were the same gardeners most reluctant to turn their backs on their old lives. While there is little to suggest that those who embraced the campaign regretted their involvement, the initial period in which gardeners prepared their plots or turned over once blooming back gardens to vegetables was often an arduous and emotional time. In 1940, Stephen Cheveley published an influential book under the title *A Garden Goes to War*. Largely a practical guide for the new grower, in several passages it evocatively captured the pain of losing those long-nurtured flower beds and lawns. Take the following words from the introduction, where he ruefully reflects on the job in hand:

We shall have to grow vegetables in our garden. It is no use thinking we can continue during the war giving so much work and thought just to keep trim lawns and fine flowers. Common sense insists that we may soon be thankful for vegetables, and conscience would never rest unless we were doing our share towards producing more food. It is saddening to look back upon the good work that has to be undone; but, after all, it is a small sacrifice, and let us hope that some day we can restore what must now be destroyed.

His stoicism is admirable but fragile. A little later, he ponders once more the imminent loss of a border in bloom: 'How ironical that when all the work and planning is bringing such a satisfying reward, we have to make a drastic changeover to growing food.' He describes how, on a Saturday afternoon in early September, he undertook the clearing of the border with his young son. 'After the first unhappy twinges of regret,' he wrote, 'we became keen on the job, and once the flowers were out of the way it didn't seem nearly so bad.' Next Cheveley explains how the peacetime gardens of the future may even benefit from their wartime change of use: 'By digging lawns now, growing vegetables and re-seeding to grass after the war, it is certain that we shall have far better lawns in the long run.' There is an irrefutable sense of a man who knows what must be done and is desperately trying to convince himself that it will all come good in the end without really believing it in his own heart of hearts.

Nor was Cheveley alone in his sadness. A 1940 advertisement for the Rototiller, a machine designed to plough up the ground and 'Do in two hours what will take a gardener perhaps a fortnight,' acknowledged what '... a melancholy sight it is to see a pleasant lawn being dug up …'. However, the need to make use of all suitable land for food production left little room for sentimentality on the part of the authorities. Margaret Todd, who was born in 1937, had grandparents who owned land near King's Lynn in Norfolk during the war. They had three tennis courts that were particularly beloved by Margaret's grand-mother. When a letter popped through the door one day from the local council telling them that they were required to dig up the courts and turn the ground over to vegetables, her grandmother was distraught to the point of heartbreak. They did what was required of them though, and grandfather took to the project with gusto, often giving home-grown vegetables away to those who had been bereaved or bombed out over the years that followed. Nonetheless, Margaret's grandmother continued to look back with regret on the loss of those tennis courts long after the war had come to an end.

Still others were wary of the testing physical labour involved. A contributor to Mass Observation noted of her husband in April 1940: 'He is all over aches and pains. Every time he gets up he groans and groans something chronic … It's them allotments as gets him.' (Mass Observation was a non-governmental research institute established in 1937, that used reports from ordinary citizens to furnish a picture of social attitudes and trends.) In *Mrs Milburn's Diaries*, edited by Peter Donnelly, the eponymous diarist was even more upfront about her dissatisfaction: 'I might as well record it – I am at the moment fed up with the garden. Every year we slave in it, take years off our life with overwork.'

The story was not all doom and gloom, though. While local authorities took responsibility for, and did a remarkable job of, identifying suitable areas to be turned into allotments, the

Ministry of Agriculture was particularly strong in securing high-profile sites. They were able to make great propaganda capital in this way and helped bond growers across all classes, from the working-class digger living in a Manchester terrace to members of the royal family and the most senior government officials.

Among the most famous images of the campaign is a photo of gardeners digging away in the soil beneath the Albert Memorial, Kensington Gardens, one of London's most recognisable land-marks. Large parts of the great parks of London were turned over to the cause at the earliest opportunity. In April 1940, William Mabane, the Parliamentary Secretary to the Ministry of Home Security, responded to a parliamentary question as to 'whether his attention has been called to the fact that, while the National Allotments Society is promoting a vigorous "dig for victory" campaign, ordinary flowers are being set out in the London parks; and will he see that these parks are used at least in part for growing food?' His response was vigorous and detailed:

> ... extensive arrangements have already been made for growing food in the Royal Parks in London. Sixty-three acres have been set aside for allotments and 80 acres are under cultivation for oats and root crops. In addition, a proportion of the greenhouse space is being used for cultivating tomatoes, lettuce and French beans, and potatoes and other vegetables are to be grown in some of the flower beds. Having regard to what has been done in this direction and to the pleasure and recreation which the parks afford to multitudes of users, my Noble Friend feels that the balance of advantage lies in not making too drastic a sacrifice of the flowers.

Indeed, there were soon rows of cabbages growing in Kensington Gardens, while Hyde Park would eventually house a piggery. There was also a spate of publicity concerning Winston Churchill's efforts to grow potatoes in his own garden.

Elsewhere, vegetable plots had been dug in the grounds of the great public museums, in the moat of the Tower of London and at the royal palaces. The grounds of Windsor Great Park were converted into what was claimed to be the largest wheat field in the country. Meanwhile, the railway companies planted up every foot of available sidings, golf courses sacrificed their fairways (though not always enthusiastically) and even the boundaries of Aintree racecourse were dug up.

The government was also able to call on several non-governmental organisations, whose spectacular efforts often went unrecognised but who were instrumental in the campaign's ultimate success. There was, arguably, no independent body more important to the campaign than the National Allotment Society (NAS), which in September 1939 agreed to 'use the whole of its machinery of organisation' to assist in the provision of more allotments, as well as to provide support and technical know-how to growers. Yet its relationship with the government was a rocky one, especially in the early months of the Second World War. The society appealed for a grant of £7,500 from the Ministry of Agriculture to carry out its work. This, they believed, was a reasonable request considering a grant of £10,000 had been awarded for similar work in the Great War. Therefore, there was a sense of shock when a Ministry of Agriculture official verbally suggested that £300 or £400 was a more likely figure. Councillor Berry of the NAS executive complained about the 'total lack of goodwill towards the National Allotment Society shown by the Ministry'.

There was also lingering resentment at the lack of action in respect of security of tenure for allotment holders since the last war. It was an issue that prompted G. W. Giles, the NAS Secretary, to write to the Ministry on 27 September 1939: 'A number of cases have arisen where land cultivated as allotments for many years is being taken either for farming or market gardening. This seems most regrettable at a time like the present …'.

Wilfred Roberts, the MP for Cumberland Northern, took up the cause in the Commons on 25 January 1940:

We get the most unfortunate instances where the work of one Minister seems to be entirely undone by that of another. An example occurs in a letter which I received from the Society of Allotment Holders. With great enthusiasm a body of allotment holders followed the Minister of Agriculture's advice to dig for victory, only to find, when they had dug and spent a lot of money, that the representatives of the Ministry of War came along, commandeered their land, and destroyed the whole of the work they had done. That sort of thing is intensely discouraging to the patriotic producer, whether he is an allotment holder or a farmer.

Fortunately, the ill-feeling between the Ministry and NAS was eventually put to bed. Giles wrote to Dorman-Smith in January 1940, '… I was directed to state that in the opinion of my Committee a much closer contact should be maintained between the organised allotment movement and your Department if the "Dig for Victory" Campaign is to achieve the object which we all so much desire,' and pointed out the 'serious gap' between the organisations. It seems a meeting was promptly arranged and in March, Giles wrote again to say that 'all misunderstandings have been cleared up. We look forward to a period of close cooperation with your Technical Division.'

Subsequently, the relationship went far more smoothly and the NAS was instrumental in seeing that allotments ran well and that growers had somewhere to turn for advice and support. It also assisted with the cooperative purchasing of seeds and equipment. The Royal Horticultural Society gave of its expertise too, not least in assisting the Ministry in the preparation of technical materials and in establishing a panel of practical gardeners across the country who could be called upon, for instance, to speak at local Dig for Victory events.

While there may not have been the rush of growers that the government hoped for, there were plenty who got involved sooner rather than later. In April 1940, the Kent Branch of the National Allotment Society met at Maidstone Town Hall to pass a resolution that typified the prevailing philosophy among growers:

> This conference, recognising that the present conflict in which our country is engaged is a war against the forces of evil which are threatening to destroy the liberties of all free peoples, pledges itself to do everything which lies in its power to defeat aggression and win through to victory. It is further of the opinion that increased home food production is an essential element if this object is to be achieved and, therefore, calls upon every patriotic citizen in the County of Kent who is able to cultivate an allotment or a garden to do so.

For a lucky few, there were unexpected rewards for early sign-up. Betty Hall lived in Lewisham in south-east London until she was evacuated at the beginning of September 1939. She left her mother behind at home, who soon heard Dorman-Smith's appeal for more allotment holders on the BBC:

> My mother, remembering the shortages in the First World War, was at the Town Hall early the following morning with the result that we had allotment No 1, Ladywell Park. Our plot faced the tennis courts (which were retained for recreational purposes) where people would watch the players or sit and have picnics. Consequently, when my father dug over the plot initially, he found quite a hoard of pennies and ha'pennies. He bought his first lot of seeds with the cash.

Meanwhile, the introduction of the famous Anderson Shelter proved an unforeseen boon for the campaign. John Anderson, a native of Edinburgh born in 1882, was a prodigiously talented scientist who had spent much of his professional life in public service, and would hold the offices of Home Secretary and Chancellor of the Exchequer during the war. First returned as an MP in 1938 for the Scottish Universities, Chamberlain had appointed him Lord Privy Seal within the year, in which role he was responsible for the implementation of air-raid precautions. Among his first actions in this capacity was to employ William Patterson, an engineer he commissioned to come up with a design for an economic and discreet bomb shelter that could easily be erected in people's back gardens.

Patterson devised plans for a construction made out of six curved and corrugated galvanised steel panels, sealed by two other steel plates. Measuring 6 foot 6 inches by 4 foot 6 inches (2 metres by 1.4 metres), it was to be half dug into the ground and camouflaged with a 15-inch layer of soil over its top. Intended to protect up to six people at a time, over 1.5 million shelters were issued to households considered most imminently under threat of attack within the first few months of the war. By late 1940, the figure had risen to over 2.25 million. The cost to the lower paid was nothing, while families in which the bread-winner pulled in more than £5 a week were expected to pay £7.

While spending any length of time in these constructions was rarely fun, as they were notably dark and damp prone, many growers recognised that they offered an ideal setting for cultivating mushrooms. Meanwhile, the layer of earth camouflaging the shelter was perfect for growing cabbages, carrots, cauliflowers, courgettes, cucumbers, marrows, rhubarb and tomatoes.

By May 1940, the war was entering a distinct new phase. Britain's disastrous attempt to assist neutral Norway in defending herself against Hitler's armies ended in ignominious retreat. The Phoney War was at an end and the performance of Neville Chamberlain and his Conservative government came under the microscope. The House of Commons hosted the 'Norway Debate' in early May, during which the former cabinet minister Leo Amery launched a scathing attack on Chamberlain's record:

> We are fighting today for our life, for our liberty, for our all; we cannot go on being led as we are. I have quoted certain words of Oliver Cromwell. I will quote certain other words. I do it with great reluctance, because I am speaking of those who are old friends and associates of mine, but they are words which, I think, are applicable to the present situation. This is what Cromwell said to the Long Parliament when he thought it was no longer fit

to conduct the affairs of the nation: 'You have sat too long here for any good you have been doing. Depart, I say, and let us have done with you. In the name of God, go.'

On 10 May 1940, Chamberlain resigned as Prime Minister and by November he was dead. Winston Churchill replaced him in Downing Street, bringing a new, magnificent focus and intensity to the execution of the war. No longer would Dig for Victory, nor any other aspect of the war, be allowed to tumble on haphazardly.

7. Blood, Toil, Tears and Sweat

Churchill addressed the House of Commons on 4 June 1940, determined to hammer home the gravity of the national position and the need for personal sacrifice:

> I would say to the House, as I said to those who have joined the Government: 'I have nothing to offer but blood, toil, tears and sweat.' We have before us an ordeal of the most grievous kind. We have before us many, many long months of struggle and of suffering ... At this time I feel entitled to claim the aid of all, and I say, 'Come, then, let us go forward together with our united strength.'

Indeed, the nation was about to experience its darkest period of the whole war. Within two months of Churchill taking office that summer, German troops had overrun Luxembourg, Holland, Belgium, Norway and France. The perilous Dunkirk evacuations happened at the end of May, the Battle of Britain began in July and Britain endured the Blitz from September. In December 1941 Churchill candidly told the US Congress that: 'If Germany had tried to invade the British Isles after the French collapse in June 1940, and if Japan had declared war on the British Empire and the United States at about the same date, no one could say what disasters and agonies might not have been our lot.'

Life for the Diggers for Victory became still tougher under such grim wartime conditions. For instance, growers suffered a lack of basic meteorological information because, in the interests of security, there were no public broadcasts of weather forecasts from the autumn of 1939 until April 1945. In addition, there were many other, more unexpected peculiarities to deal with. Margaret Todd, while still a very young girl, was allowed to help on the family veg patch and remembers being tormented by long slivers of silver paper that were all but impossible to remove entirely from the soil no matter how much raking and picking out she did. These were strips of metallic foil, some 6 to 8 inches in length, that were dropped over England by the planes of the Luftwaffe with the intention of causing interference to Britain's radio receivers and radar systems. That they would be an annoyance to the nation's gardeners would surely have been an unexpected but welcome additional consequence for the regime in Berlin.

Other growers, though, had more serious threats to deal with, not the least of which were enemy bombs. The Rev. Peter Turner recalled how his father dealt with an incendiary bomb that fell close to the family property during the Bath Blitz of 1942. The house stood on a hill and at the end of the back garden was a high wall, at the bottom of which sat the device. Mr Turner quickly scaled down the wall and then hurriedly buried the bomb in a neighbouring garden. The Turners' own garden could not be used as it was then playing home to a colony of rabbits kept under wire mesh. When the neighbour awoke to discover that his cabbage patch had been dug out he was, Peter remembers, 'most miffed'.

With the need to significantly increase domestic production never more pressing, the government continued to concentrate not on the Diggers for Victory, but on the commercial agricultural sector. While a battalion of keen amateurs could make a truly valuable contribution, all their efforts would be in vain if the farms failed to take up their challenge. Fortunately, the professionals were equal to the job and, through initiatives like the 'ploughing-up' campaigns and rapid improvements in technical functioning, helped compensate for a drop in food imports of more than half the pre-war levels.

Traditional food supply routes, as expected, came under intense pressure. Fears about the threat posed to shipping by German submarines proved entirely justified. Over 2,400 British merchant vessels were lost to enemy actions over the duration of the war (275 in March 1942 alone), with 30,000 merchant seamen sacrificing their lives. By the end of 1941 Churchill's government calculated that it would be unable to import more than 15.5 million tons of food per annum. As it transpired, imports would not get over 12 million tons a year for the remainder of the conflict.

By the time of the Dunkirk evacuation in May and June 1940, the European trading network had already been disrupted beyond recognition. With imports ceasing from the occupied countries of Europe, the United Kingdom lost out on some 1.75 million tons of food that it might otherwise have expected to import. There would be some gains elsewhere, notably from the nations of the British Empire, from whom imports (food and non-food combined) increased in value terms from less that £550 million (circa £15.75 billion today) in 1939 to almost

£800 million (circa £23 billion today) in 1944. Still, there was a downside to relying on imports from further away. For instance, Australian wheat imports were crucial to plug the hole in UK stocks but the crop often did not last the long journey halfway round the globe very well.

The USA and Canada also traded and donated provisions that helped keep the population fed, and in July 1941 President Franklin Roosevelt authorised the Lend-Lease Agreement. Under its terms the USA agreed to ship food and other essential supplies to the United Kingdom on a deferred payment system and in return for the use of certain strategically important regions and territories. In short, it was an effective blank cheque for Britain until the agreement ended in September 1945, without which the country would in all likelihood have been unable to see the war through to a successful conclusion.

Addressing the Commons on 17 April 1945 after the death of Roosevelt, Churchill referred to '... the extraordinary measure of assistance called Lend-Lease, which will stand forth as the most unselfish and unsordid financial act of any country in all history'. The outcome for the United Kingdom was that it only finished paying off its Second World War debts to Washington in December 2006, but few doubt that the consequences would have been catastrophic without the Lend-Lease Agreement and subsequent American post-war reconstruction loans.

Yet for all the overseas assistance, by 1943–4 the nation was importing a fraction of the food that it had five years earlier, a situation it could only endure as a result of the increases in domestic production. By 1944, the total area under cultivation had increased to 19.8 million acres from 12.9 million acres in 1939. The 'ploughing-up' campaigns at the start of the war had laid the foundations. By the end of the war, wheat production had increased by 36 per cent, greens by 50 per cent, cereals by 66 per cent and potatoes by 80 per cent. Where the country had been able to feed itself without external supplies for 120 days of the year in 1939, by 1945 it could see itself through 160 days.

Although farming was one of the reserved occupations, the industry nonetheless achieved its increased production despite some 100,000 farm labourers receiving their call-ups to the armed services. The shortfall was made up for by a number of means. By the end of the war there were 58,000 prisoners of war working on the land. Civilians also contributed by signing up for 'working holidays', getting paid a nominal wage to help with vital agricultural work in the 'Lend a Hand on the Land' scheme. Joan Strange was one of these holiday-makers, spending the summer of 1943 on a paid holiday at the Agricultural Workers' Camp at Ampthill, Bedfordshire. In September 1943, civil servants were offered a week's special leave if they agreed to use it to help with bringing in the harvest. Somewhere between 60,000 and 70,000 children also went on farm camp holidays that year, while schools and other youth organisations such as the Scouts offered their assistance too.

But the single most important group in keeping the farms ticking over was the Women's Land Army (WLA), which at its peak in 1944 boasted more than 80,000 members. The first incarnation of the WLA had appeared in 1917, set up by Lady Trudie Denman, a philanthropist from the ranks of the aristocracy, at the behest of the Minister of Agriculture, Roland Prothero. The members of the WLA had undertaken whatever tasks were required of them, from milking cows to repairing thatches, shepherding to driving tractors, and by November 1918 there were 23,000 women signed up.

Lady Denman was approached by the Ministry of Agriculture in 1938 with an invitation to head up a women's branch within the department. She was by then also Chairman of the Family Planning Association and of the National Federation of Women's Institutes. She oversaw the rebirth of the WLA in July 1939, proclaiming: 'The Land Army fights in the fields. It is in the fields of Britain that the most critical battle of the present war may well be fought and won.'

Membership was open to females over seventeen years of age, and recruits were expected to work a basic forty-eight-hour week (or fifty hours during summer and at other critical periods). The women were employed not as government workers but as employees of individual farms, and their terms were often harsh. An average weekly wage was 25 shillings, considerably less than the 38 shillings paid to their male counterparts, who themselves received below the national average. Typically, half of this income went straight back to the employers to cover board and lodging; nor was there a statutory holiday allowance.

There was little glamour in being attached to the WLA, from the uniform of baggy brown corduroy breeches, fawn socks up to the knee, a fawn Aertex blouse and a green V-neck jumper, to the work the women were expected to undertake. If you were lucky you might be set to milking or ploughing, but you might equally find yourself on rat-catching duty or be asked to castrate the pigs. They must have been eye-opening times for a large part of the membership, many of whom were drawn from the towns and cities (about a third of members hailed from London alone) and would have been entirely green in the ways of the countryside.

There was also the tricky issue of preserving the honour of

young women sent off to live in strange places on their own. In October 1939, a Glamorgan county agricultural director suggested a 9 p.m. curfew for WLA girls, claiming that, 'It is alleged the conduct of some land girls after working hours is a public scandal.' Lady Denham leapt to their defence: 'The reports we have received from all over the country say not only that the Land Girls' progress is extremely good, but that their standard of conduct is excellent.' Over time, though, many of the women moved out of their digs on the farms and into shared hostels nearby.

The reality of WLA membership was a far cry from the image portrayed on the recruiting posters, which typically featured a glamorous young thing in a jodhpurs-and-jersey combo, wistfully staring out into the distance over a proud field of golden wheat. Indeed, one of the campaign's poster girls reported a serious falling-out with her father after allowing herself to be photographed for a publicity shot with the top buttons of her blouse daringly undone. There was also a stirring official song:

> Back to the land, we must all lend a hand.
> To the farms and the field we must go.
> There's a job to be done,
> Though we can't fire a gun
> We can still do our bit with the hoe.
> When your muscles are strong
> You will soon get along
> And you'll think the country life's grand;
> We're all needed now,
> We must all speed the plough
> So come with us – Back to the Land.

It was, alas, ripe for corruption by aficionados of innuendo, who reworked the song as 'Backs to the Land'.

Initial membership numbers were on the disappointing side, standing at only 7,000 by August 1940, but then rapidly grew to their 1944 high. By the time the movement was disbanded in 1950, over 100,000 members had passed through the organisation, having more than adequately covered the farm labourers lost to conscription. Attempts to bring the WLA into the Dig for Victory campaign were given short shrift, though. In 1943 the Domestic Food Production Sub-Committee of the Buckinghamshire War Ag. summarised the situation:

> The Women's Land Army is in no case allowed to supply members for work in private gardens unless their work was 80 per cent essential food production … The object of the Ministry of Agriculture is to encourage food production in allotments and gardens where the owners could themselves undertake the labour, but to discourage it where labour has to be acquired from outside.

After the war, there was a quite scandalous lack of recognition for the WLA's contribution to the national effort. Only in 2007 did the Department of the Environment, Food and Rural Affairs (a successor to the Ministry of Agriculture) announce that over 30,000 members of the WLA and the Women's Timber Corps (known as 'Lumber Jills') would receive commemorative badges. One of these recipients in 2008 was Mary Chauncy, who had joined the WLA in April 1942 and was demobbed in January 1946. She worked on the Floral Mile, on the main road between London and Reading renowned for its horticulture, where she became staunch friends with five of her colleagues.

'The gang', as they were known, agreed to meet annually, health permitting, and its three remaining members continue to do so. 'I had a very happy time in the WLA,' said Mary, but it is clearly a frustration for her that only in 2000 was the organisation granted a position in the Remembrance Day parade at the Cenotaph, Whitehall, when many of her friends were no longer around to share the experience. Had the commercial agricultural sector failed to meet its production challenges, the efforts of the Diggers for Victory would have been for nothing. The WLA was essential to those goals being reached and, for their essential work, the women deserved better.

As for those considering taking up the spade in an amateur capacity, there was no greater incentive than the ongoing challenges posed by rationing. The public proved to be remarkably tolerant of the system, as long as they considered it was administered fairly, and responded well to Churchill's position of 'honesty is the best policy'. He told Parliament on 10 June 1941, 'The British nation is unique in this respect. They are the only people who like to be told how bad things are, who like to be told the worst.'

A report by the Home Intelligence Division of the Ministry of Information came to a similar conclusion in a report from March 1942: 'It seems clear that people are willing to bear any sacrifice, if a 100 per cent effort can be reached and the burden fairly borne by all.' The Ministry of Food's campaign to win over public opinion included a quote supposedly from a real-life butcher: 'And then there's this trying to wangle a bit extra to the ration. It's asking me to get into trouble, but that's not the worst of it. It's downright selfish and it's downright unpatriotic. Giving a helping hand to Hitler, that's what I call it.'

But the basic ration made for an incredibly dull diet. Though the exact composition of the ration varied as food stocks fluctuated, a typical weekly allowance for an adult might have included:

4 ounces of bacon,
2 ounces of butter,
2 ounces of cheese,
1 fresh egg,
1 packet of dried egg per family per month,
2 ounces of lard,
5 ounces of margarine,
1s. 2d. worth of meat,
2½ pints of milk,
8 ounces of sugar,
3 ounces of sweets
and a ¼ pound of tea.

From 1942, the National Loaf became the staple food, essentially a high-nutrition wholemeal loaf with a slightly off-putting greyish tinge. It was much loathed by a nation that loved its white bread, especially as retailers were required to sell it a day after baking on the basis that if it was sold in its freshest state, people would be less likely to regulate their consumption. A slightly stale, day-old slice of the National Loaf tended to be quite enough for anyone.

In an attempt to keep diets at least a little varied, the population did their best to embrace a range of new foods including Spam and whale meat. Housewives became used to sacrificing a large chunk of their week to stand in lines in the hope of getting hold of something to perk up their dinner table.

As a respondent from Hull told Mass Observation in 1941: 'It is hysteria with some people – whenever they see a long queue they just join on the end.'

Thus, the advantages for those willing to spend some of their spare time working the soil were obvious. Churchill was open with the people about the precariousness of the nation's position but built a sense that the situation could be turned around by unity of purpose, hard work, courage and good humour. In such conditions the Dig for Victory campaign was set to bloom. On 27 April 1941, Churchill broadcast on the BBC, painting a vivid picture of the national mood:

I was asked last week whether I was aware of some uneasiness which it was said existed in the country on account of the gravity, as it was described, of the war situation. So I thought it would be a good thing to go and see for myself what this 'uneasiness' amounted to, and I went to some of our great cities and seaports which had been most heavily bombed, and to some of the places where the poorest people had got it worst. I have come back not only reassured, but refreshed ... It is quite true that I have seen many painful scenes of havoc, and of fine buildings and acres of cottage homes blasted into rubble-heaps of ruin. But it is just in those very places where the malice of the savage enemy has done its worst, and where the ordeal of the men, women and children has been most severe, that I found their morale most high and splendid ... The British nation is stirred and moved as it has never been at any time in its long, eventful, famous history, and it is no hackneyed trope of speech to say that they mean to conquer or to die.

8. New Brooms

Despite the apparent potential of Reginald Dorman-Smith and William Morrison, neither man had led their respective ministries with the energy and efficiency that they might have done, especially in respect of Dig for Victory. Dorman-Smith should be credited with having overseen a successful ploughing-up campaign and instigating other vital initiatives, such as building up a reserve of 3,000 tractors. However his department had simply not managed to capture the imaginations of enough back-garden and allotment planters. As the next couple of years would prove, they were out there but Dorman-Smith was not the man to entice them. Meanwhile, Morrison had tied himself up in knots as he attempted to calm fears over food shortages at a time of immense social upheaval.

When Winston Churchill formed his wartime cabinet in 1940, he moved both men on; Dorman-Smith would become Governor General of Burma and Morrison Postmaster-General. They were replaced by Robert Hudson and Frederick, Lord Woolton, respectively, who proved to be a far more dynamic duo. Under their joint guidance, the Dig for Victory campaign really ignited.

Hudson was a Londoner born in 1886 who had won for himself a reputation for hard work and competence during stints at the Ministry of Shipping and the Department of Overseas Trade. With his urban background and distinctly non-agricultural government experience, Hudson could not claim like his predecessor to be a 'farming man'. Yet of the two, it is he who is regarded as the greater success. His energy, eloquence and hunger for work proved irresistible, particularly when united with the gifts possessed by Lord Woolton.

Woolton may have received his knighthood in 1935 and made a personal fortune as a businessman but he also possessed an unerring common touch. Born Frederick James Marquis in Salford in 1883 to staunchly ambitious, middle-class parents, he qualified as a maths teacher and taught at Burnley Grammar School while undertaking further academic studies into labour mobility and poverty. He was appointed as an economics research fellow at Manchester University in 1910, receiving his MA two years later and participating in a range of social projects. Declared unfit for active service in the First World War, he joined the War Office's Requisition Department and, later, the Leather Control Board. His social work had previously brought him into contact with the Lewis family, owners of a famous Liverpool department store. In 1920, Woolton joined the firm, becoming a well-known commercial figure, firstly in the region and eventually throughout the nation. Invited to serve on a range of influential government committees during the 1920s and 1930s, he remained non-partisan at the time of his knighthood.

He was a vociferous critic of Chamberlain's appeasement policy, and the two had a fierce run-in when Woolton pulled German products from Lewis's after the annexation of Austria in 1938. Nonetheless, in 1939 he was brought in as an advisor to the Secretary of State for War, Leslie Hore-Belisha, and asked to focus on the practicalities of how to keep the armed forces clothed in the event of hostilities. Chamberlain then granted Woolton a peerage so that he would be able to assume high office. Woolton was geared up to become Lord Windermere until his wife vetoed the choice because of its Wildean connotations and persuaded him to settle on Woolton instead.

On taking over at the Ministry of Food, Woolton was well known among the political and mercantile classes but recognition of him in the country at large was not widespread. However, he was to become a regular and familiar voice on the airwaves, dispensing timely advice on food and nutrition throughout the Second World War so that by its end, only Churchill could claim greater popularity with the public among members of the government. Woolton came to the Ministry of Food with an agenda. Having witnessed the poverty that prevailed among large parts of the population, and having undertaken academic studies in the areas of poverty and ill health, he was determined to use his position to improve the lot of the poor. As he would later write in his memoirs, he fixed on using 'the powers of a wartime Ministry of Food to make provision for the health of children ... [and] stamp out the diseases that arose from malnutrition'.

Both Hudson and Woolton had the sense to surround themselves with highly capable personnel, benefitting them personally and the nation as a whole. At the Ministry of Agriculture, Hudson could turn to his deputy, Tom Williams (later Baron Williams of Barnburgh). Born in Blackwell, Derbyshire, in 1888, he was the tenth of fourteen children, though three of his siblings did not survive beyond infancy. The son of a miner, Williams finished his formal education at the age of eleven and found employment at the local colliery. A lifelong trade unionist, his difficult upbringing naturally put him on the side of the poor and deprived, a stance that put him in harmony with Woolton despite their own class divide. Williams realised that the war offered a great opportunity to revitalise the agricultural industry and bring it out of the moribund state that had dominated for most of the 1930s. Furthermore, while his own background was in mining, he was a working man to whom farmers (so often distrusting of the posh nobs who mostly ran government) were able to relate. While the Ministry wielded significant wartime statutory powers, Williams sought to work by compromise and negotiation, doing much to soften and popularise Hudson's tenure. Williams ultimately succeeded Hudson as Minister at the end of the war and played a pivotal role in the creation of the 1947 Agricultural Act. When Williams published his autobiography *Digging for Britain* in 1965, it included a foreword by Clement Atlee. The great post-war Labour Prime Minister wrote that Williams had 'effected nothing less than a revolution in British agriculture,' and that 'his place in history is assured as the greatest British Minister of Agriculture of all time'.

Over at the Ministry of Food, Lord Woolton (who as a non-partisan was a highly effective mediator between Labour and Conservative colleagues) had not only the ear of Sir John Boyd Orr to bend but also that of Professor Jack Drummond, who was instrumental in the successful roll-out of the rationing system. Drummond had spent much of the 1930s undertaking an intensive study of 500 years of domestic eating habits that was published in 1939 as *The Englishman's Food*. He was brought into the Ministry of Food at the onset of war to advise on the implications of wide-scale gas contamination of food supplies. By February 1941, Drummond was the Ministry's leading scientific adviser and had developed a strong relationship with Woolton, devising a programme of rationing that was acceptable to the public once the gravity of Britain's food situation had been grasped by the proverbial man (and housewife) on the street.

Churchill and Woolton also shared the view that the development of a canteen culture would help guarantee access to nutritionally balanced meals for ever-greater numbers of people. Restaurants were deemed 'off ration' at the outset of the war, so those who were rich enough and used to eating out continued to do so, dining much as they ever did to the chagrin of many, until restrictions were finally put in place some way into the war. However, the vast majority of the country was, historically, outside of restaurant culture and had always dined within the domestic setting. Woolton was determined to change that. Robert Boothby, who served as Woolton's Permanent Secretary, said, 'It is cheaper – and better – to eat together ... Lord Woolton had expressed interest in the development of communal feeding not only as a wartime measure, but also as a long-term policy – a permanent and beneficial feature of national life in Britain.'

Companies employing over certain numbers of people were required to provide economical and healthy meals for their employees, and canteens became an increasingly common feature of life. Meanwhile, between 1939 and 1945, schools registered a 700 per cent increase in the provision of free meals to pupils. In 1940, as the Blitz took hold, the London County Council set up a number of both permanent and temporary sites to provide food to people whose homes had been bombed. These formed the basis of what became a national network of not-for-profit 'British Restaurants', run by the Ministry of Food for anyone to eat in. The name 'British Restaurants' was put forward by Churchill in favour of the original suggestion, 'Communal Feeding Centres', which he considered 'an odious expression, suggestive of communism and the workhouse'.

The restaurants served wholesome food at eminently affordable prices. You could get a tea or coffee for 1½d., soup for 2d., a plate of meat and two veg for 8d., and a pudding for 3d., none of which came off the ration. By September 1943, there were some 2,160 British Restaurants, providing upwards of 600,000 meals each day, at locations as various as the Victora & Albert Museum in London and Bath's grand Pump Room to local Scout huts and abandoned warehouses. By the end of the war, over half the population had dined in one of these eateries at least once, and though the food may not have been Michelin star standard, it was decent enough and set a benchmark for cheap, mass catering. Between 1939 and 1945, the total number of work canteens increased from around 1,500 to 18,500, and 10 per cent of all meals were being taken in public settings. Britain had become a nation that ate out.

Along with Wilson Jameson at the Ministry of Health, Woolton, Drummond and Boyd Orr were credited with ensuring huge leaps in the nation's nutritional health during the war, delivering hard-hitting messages that emphasised the value of well-prepared home-grown produce and which were vital in putting wind into the sails of the Dig for Victory movement. Indeed, in 1947, the Lasker Awards committee of the American Public Health Association would cite the combined wartime efforts of the Ministries of Food and Health as 'one of the greatest demonstrations in public health administration that the world has ever seen'. It is a sad footnote that the considerable achievements of Professor Drummond's life were to be over-shadowed by the sad circumstances surrounding his murder, along with his wife and ten-year-old daughter, while they were on a camping holiday in Provence in 1952. A mystery that was never solved.

The figure at the Ministry of Food with arguably the greatest direct influence on the Dig for Victory campaign was Professor John Raeburn. Born in Kirkcaldy in 1912, he was schooled at Manchester Grammar before leaving for Edinburgh University. Aged twenty-four, he went to China where he took up the position of Professor of Agricultural Economics at Nanking University. He stayed for barely a year before fleeing back to Britain at the start of the Second Sino-Japanese War in 1937. He found a job at the University of Oxford before signing on as a statistician at the Ministry of Food in 1939. By 1941, Raeburn had been appointed as chief of the Agricultural Plans Branch, which was by then based in North Wales. He was effectively Dig for Victory's 'man at the Ministry' and the main go-between with the Ministry of Agriculture. He stayed in position until the end of the war (outlasting Woolton who left for pastures new in 1943), and won the respect of all those who worked with him for his championing of the campaign. Known to his colleagues as J.R. (his middle name was Ross), he was never one to suffer fools gladly and could be decidedly stern, but was also honest and straightforward and, importantly, lived what he preached: he spent much of his spare time tending his own garden, growing fruit and veg to boost the rations of his own family.

This wholesale change of key personnel after Churchill became Prime Minister in 1940 made an immediate impact on Dig for Victory. In bringing new blood to the ministries, Churchill's decisive and prompt action (characteristic of his entire wartime tenure) doubtless saved Dig for Victory from an ignominious reputation. Instead of becoming an under-funded, amateurish if well-meaning incidental to the war, Churchill helped propel it towards its status as one of the great Home Front campaigns.

Of course, even under Woolton and Hudson there remained some thorny issues with which to get to grips. One such question was what should be done to keep market gardens and the country's larger houses still producing at their optimum levels where professional gardening staff had been called up to the services. While this was, by its nature, an issue for a relatively small proportion of the participants in Digging for Victory, it affected those properties which had the potential to be among the most significant contributors to the nation's stores.

Some landowners needed more encouragement than others to participate. It was an oft-heard complaint that many mansion gardens seemed to carry on as if the war was simply not happening, filling their beds and glasshouses with flowers where vegetables might have flourished. In August 1940, a newspaper article was published praising the efforts of the owner of a grand house in Loughton, Essex. He is spoken of in heroic terms that surely would have left no householder in a similar situation unstirred:

> An excellent example of how owners of fairly large gardens may help towards the success of the 'Dig for Victory' campaign is to be found here in a delightful corner of the Prime Minister's constituency ... Here in Essex Mr C.F. Clark, of Ripley Grange, has given a lead that is sure to be followed in other parts of the country. Ripley Grange may be said to rejoice in its beautiful

gardens. Until the war came, the cultivation of vegetables had no part in the scheme of this well-planned estate. Then, thinking first of the wives and families of Service men, Mr Clark decided to sacrifice a large part of his garden to vegetable production ... The wives of many Service men in the district are greatly indebted to Mr Clark for the fresh produce they have received. He is now sending vegetables to local schools and hospitals and a scheme is being prepared under which the London Hospital may benefit ... Perhaps Mr Clark's greatest reward for his public-spirited endeavour is the receipt of schoolchildren's letters of thanks.

Some landowners warned against a 'brain drain' of professional gardeners that they claimed would have been unthinkable among workers in other essential fields. Throughout the land, they argued, were large gardens long tended by skilled experts to be as productive as possible. And yet, just as the nation most needed their productivity, vital gardening staff were being called up. In a letter to *The Times* on 25 February 1941, Lieutenant-Colonel J.H. Westley outlined the problem:

My gardener received this morning a week's notice to join an infantry training centre of a county regiment other than his own. He is a skilled gardener, aged thirty-two, height 5ft 1in, eyesight defective. I know that the needs of private individuals, however large and productive their gardens may be, must give way to all other considerations in wartime, but surely there is no sense in making an infantry soldier of a man whose skill, if properly utilised in the public service, could produce extra food for a large number of the population.

That same month, Lord Bingley – experienced on the front line of politics since becoming an MP in 1906 – raised the issue in the House of Lords:

> There is, I believe, a special opportunity of increasing home food production by the cultivation of the gardens of the country, large and small, and I hope that the Ministry of Labour or whichever Government Department is concerned will be very careful not to deplete unduly the supply of trained gardeners. There are, in a good many places, glasshouses of various kinds which at other times are devoted to the growing of flowers and grapes and other luxuries, and the owners of them will be perfectly ready to let them be used for more necessary things. A great deal can be got out of them if they are properly managed, but the ordinary unskilled labourer turned into them for the first time is not going to be of much use in producing real results …
>
> We are told that old men and girls can be employed, but that is not the same thing. I believe that efforts to increase home production of food will be seriously handicapped unless something is done about keeping skilled men who can really do the job … Girls are not going to be so easy to get as some people think. There is a great demand for them for munitions making. A certain element of fashion enters into this. It is rather the fashion for a girl to go into a munitions factory in preference to getting up at any hour of the morning to feed animals in the dark on a dirty, muddy farm. That is not a very attractive job for girls who have been employed in town surroundings. Girls have been doing splendid work, but we must face the fact that there is a shortage.

Inflexible legislation offered little hope of solving this complex question and was never a real option. The calling up of vast numbers of the general population would inevitably throw up anomalies and injustices. While no one wanted to strip the country of its essential skilled labour, any attempts to institute regulations allowing the richest landowners to keep hold of their valued staff while other families watched as their fathers, sons and brothers went off to war would have been damagingly divisive. A much more appealing remedy was for the relevant authorities to take a pragmatic approach on a case-by-case basis. There would still be the odd mistake or questionable decision, but it offered the best chance of alleviating the problem without unnecessarily turning it into a national debate on class privilege.

In early March 1941, J.F. Ramsbotham shared his experiences in a published letter. Confronted by the prospect of losing his experienced head gardener, he had paid a visit to the local labour exchange, where he was informed that there were no suitable replacements on their books and little prospect that there would be at any point in the short to medium term. He thus undertook the administrative task of securing a certificate of reservation, exempting his man from a call-up. 'I hate the word "influence," which has been a curse to the country,' wrote Ramsbotham, 'and I used none, but I do think that every person should be employed to the best advantage of our truly great country, and it is my opinion that the Westmorland Agricultural Executive Committee used their judgement wisely.'

There were, though, additional complications that faced a great many large houses and impacted on their ability to contribute to the Dig for Victory campaign. Chief among these was the transfer of wartime control of private country houses from their original owners to the military. It was a question that occupied the mind of one F.H. Mitchell of Crowborough, who exercised his thoughts on the subject in what proved to be a coliseum for popular debate, the letters page of *The Times*. On 25 March 1941, he wrote:

> Unfortunately when owners go, gardeners go too. Consequently a very large number of kitchen gardens have been neglected for many months and will very soon become infested with weeds … The remedy seems simple, for surely soldiers who are billeted in these houses would be only too willing to dig for victory in their spare time …

It was indeed a neat solution, and one which found favour with many, though by no means all, of the troops in question. Over the course of the war, the armed services proved highly adept at producing food from the soil, not only in the relative comfort of requisitioned country houses, but in the more mundane settings of permanent military bases too.

Some problems, though, seemed to have no such straightforward solution. The treatment of aliens in wartime was a particularly fraught issue. On 4 June 1940, Churchill admitted as much to the House of Commons:

> We have found it necessary to take measures of increasing stringency, not only against enemy aliens and suspicious characters of other nationalities, but also against British subjects who may become a danger or a nuisance should the war be transported to the United Kingdom. I know there are a great many people affected by the orders which we have made who are the passionate enemies of Nazi Germany. I am very sorry for them, but we cannot, at the present time and under the present stress, draw all the distinctions which we should like to do.

G. W. Radford shared the details of a particularly sad case with his fellow *Times* readers in June 1940:

> As a reader in the Ruislip-Northwood district, which has recently been declared a protected area, I am at a loss to understand the expulsion of all friendly aliens from that area ... To cite my own case, I turned over part of my garden to vegetables, and employed a friendly alien to work on this food production. A Jew of some sixty years of age, he was happy to work with his hands in what he termed the common cause. His son, who could have in the early days of the war proceeded to the United States, considered it his duty to join up in the Auxiliary Military Pioneer Corps. A fine type of young Jew, who has already suffered the tortures of the concentration camp, his one aim in life was to do something to combat Hitlerism and all it stands for. His wife worked as a domestic, and thereby released my wife for very active participation in local defence work. I am a member of the Local Defence Volunteers. Now what is the position? The home must be kept going, so local defence work is minus one. Do I withdraw from the Local Defence Volunteers in order to dig for victory or let the vegetable plot fade out? ... Truly the working of the bureaucratic mind passeth all understanding.

As if to prove that final point, once in office, Winston Churchill decided on a clear-out at the misfiring Ministry of Information, whose effective working would be essential to the success of Dig for Victory. John Reith was unceremoniously removed to the Ministry of Transport, he and Churchill having waged a long-running feud since Reith had resisted Churchill's attempt to wrest control of the BBC for the government during the General Strike of 1926.

Unfortunately, the Ministry remained as prone as ever to entirely misread the public mood even after Churchill installed Duff Cooper as Reith's replacement. Tommy Handley, the Liverpudlian superstar of BBC radio's *It's That Man Again*, did a much better job of chiming with popular opinion when he christened it the 'Ministry of Aggravation'. Cooper, who was Eton and Oxford educated, had first entered the Commons in 1924 and had served variously as Financial Secretary to the War Office, Financial Secretary to the Treasury and Secretary of State for War. He became First Lord of the Admiralty in May 1937 but fell out with Chamberlain over the appeasement policy, leading him into a close alliance with Churchill. Cooper's attack against the Munich Agreement, which he considered dishonourable, saw him resume his career on the back benches in late 1938 but he had been clever enough to see that the balance of power had turned inexorably in Churchill's favour.

When Churchill took up residence in Downing Street, he appointed Cooper despite his old ally being reluctant to take up the reins. While the Ministry was undoubtedly starting to find its feet, Cooper brought with him a notably bad relationship with the newspapers. Tensions were not lessened by Cooper's eagerness to take advantage of the work of the Mass Observation Unit, which used diary reports from citizens to furnish a picture of social attitudes and trends. Officials from that organisation became known as 'Cooper's Snoopers'.

Cooper nonetheless held the office until July 1941, when he was replaced by Brendan Bracken, who came through the Ministry like a proverbial breath of fresh air and stayed until May 1945. Born in County Tipperary in 1901, he had a background in both politics and journalism, which immediately marked him out as a suitable man for the job in hand. He was a character for whom the description 'larger than life' might have been invented, and was not to everybody's taste. A blaze of orange hair framed his pale face, a pair of wire spectacles perched on his flat nose and his smile revealed a set of badly preserved gnashers, which were further discoloured by his prodigious smoking habit. He spoke with a strange hybrid accent that seemed to pay homage to his Irish roots with, to some ears, elements of Cockney and Australian thrown in for good measure.

Bracken had a long-standing friendship with Churchill, during both the good times and bad of Churchill's career. They would drink and talk together long into the night, and Churchill admired his friend's ability to make things happen. When, in September 1939, Chamberlain brought Churchill back into government as First Lord of the Admiralty, Bracken was installed as his Parliamentary Private Secretary, from which position he did much to pave the way for Churchill's ascent to the premiership.

On arriving at the Ministry of Information, Bracken set about ridding the department of its tendency towards jingoistic didacticism which he knew did not play well with the public. Instead, it would start to produce straightforward and useful information, while trusting the public to respond to it in the right way. It was a change of attitude that liberated both the Ministry and the public, breaking down the wall of mutual distrust that had inhibited both sides up to that point. He also took the bold decision of adopting a more hands-off approach towards the BBC and its domestic broadcasting. This was grist to the mill for the Dig for Victory campaign. Having revolutionised the Ministry of Information, Bracken soon tired of the minutiae of running the department and from 1943 spent most of his time as a general advisor to Churchill. Day-to-day running of the Ministry fell to Cyril Radcliffe, its Director-General, who effectively maintained its health for the duration of the war.

The Ministries of Agriculture and Food, bursting with ideas that they wanted to communicate, at last had access to an organ with the infrastructures and technical know-how to really do them justice. Hudson and Woolton worked closely with the Ministry of Information's Home Publicity Division, Campaign Division and the General Production Division, the latter of which became capable of producing posters, exhibition materials and the like far quicker than any of its commercial competitors. It was a bonus for the creatives at the Ministry of Information that they could turn to Hudson, Woolton and, on occasion, Churchill to assist with direct addresses. When the Prime Minister himself declared that, 'Every endeavour must be made to grow the greatest volume of food of which this fertile land is capable,' the public was sure to listen.

DIG FOR VICTORY

The defining image of the campaign and the subject of an enduring and intriguing mystery – just whose foot is on the spade?
The Advertising Archives

Above: Food shortages ensured that queuing became a national pastime during the War.
Imperial War Museum

Above and right: Some young recruits to the Garden Army, who prospered under the guidance of the remarkable Bethnal Green Bombed Sites Association.
Tower Hamlets Local History Library and Archive

Queen Elizabeth inspected the work going on at Bethnal Green in London in June 1943.
Tower Hamlets Local History Library and Archive

London's royal parks offered a fine backdrop against which to grow your veg (a job one could do while still looking stylish!).
Imperial War Museum

The Ministry of Information established a fine roster of artists, who employed a wide range of styles and techniques to hammer home their stirring messages. Meanwhile, among the flood of Dig for Victory-related literature that emerged, few volumes were as magnificently titled as Charles Wysegardner's *Cloches versus Hitler*.

.. every available piece of land must be cultivated

GROW YOUR OWN FOOD
supply your own cookhouse

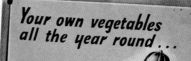

USE SPADES NOT SHIPS

GROW YOUR OWN FOOD
AND SUPPLY YOUR OWN COOKHOUSE

*Above: The Advertising Archives;
below left: The Garden Museum;
below right: Getty Images*

Cloches
versus
Hitler

by
CHARLES WYSE-GARDNER

A SIMPLE GUIDE
TO
INTENSIVE VEGETABLE CULTURE

PRICE
3 D.

Your own vegetables
all the year round ...

if you

DIG FOR
VICTORY NOW

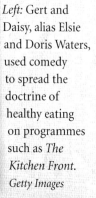

Left: A young Michael Foot, future leader of the Labour Party, coined the Dig for Victory slogan in an editorial for the *London Evening Standard* in 1939.
Getty Images

Below: Rob Hudson (right), the Minster of Agriculture from 1940, formed a potent partnership with his opposite number at the Ministry of Food, Lord Woolton.
Getty Images

Left: Gert and Daisy, alias Elsie and Doris Waters, used comedy to spread the doctrine of healthy eating on programmes such as *The Kitchen Front*.
Getty Images

Right: Lord Woolton, the avuncular Minister of Food, whose iron will to improve the nation's nutrition was key to the campaign's success.
Getty Images

Left: Dig for Victory offered those unable to serve in the armed forces the chance to make a real contribution to the war effort.
Imperial War Museum

Below: German gardeners growing produce in the shadow of the bombed-out Reichstag Building after the fall of Berlin.
Getty Images

Mr Middleton (left), the popular BBC gardening broadcaster and font of knowledge for millions of amateur growers. Seen here inspecting an inviting display of vegetables at a horticultural show in Nottingham, his first love always remained flowers. A colleague would later note of him: 'He could not love an onion where a dahlia might grow'.

Getty Images

Design: www.timpeters.co.uk

9. The Trade, the Town and the Country

Despite the energetic and largely effective leaderships of Hudson and Woolton, precise boundaries of jurisdiction between their two departments were never entirely established. This confusion was neatly exemplified by the case of the Domestic Produce Advisory Council.

The Ministry of Agriculture had incorporated an Allotments Advisory Committee since 1922. It was an influential body that did much to press the cause of allotment holders and vigorously campaigned for better security of tenure both before and during the war. While it was a representative body and included members from leading allotment organisations throughout the land, it was not designed to provide the 'nuts and bolts' advice that the civil servants needed to guide Dig for Victory. Therefore, in February 1940 the Ministry began to put together plans to establish a Council of Produce from Allotments and Private Gardens, which was quickly replaced by the Domestic Produce Advisory Council (with a dedicated Allotments and Gardens Committee).

Under the chairmanship of Lord Bingley (with its Scottish branch chaired by Sir Robert Grieg), the Council had a wide-ranging, highly skilled and experienced membership drawn from leading national bodies as disparate as the Accredited Poultry Breeders' Federation, the National Farmers' Union and the Society of Friends. Rooted within the Ministry of Agriculture, it was nonetheless run in partnership with the Ministry of Food and reported to both bodies. Where the subject of food production overlapped into food distribution was often vague, so communication channels were regularly unclear. This blurring of responsibilities resulted in a curious situation: while it was Hudson, the Minister of Agriculture, who represented Dig for Victory throughout the war, in the popular collective memory Dig for Victory is eternally associated more with Woolton at the Ministry of Food.

Despite this, the fuzziness concerning the role of each department had little impact on the day-to-day running of Dig for Victory or its overall success. However, there was one vexed question that occupied the minds of growers and administrators alike for the duration of the war and was never resolved to any satisfactory degree. This concerned the disposal of excess produce from non-commercial gardeners and allotment holders. Was excess produce principally a problem of production (that is to say, should growers be encouraged *not* to grow a surplus) or one of distribution (it being unreasonable to run a food production campaign in which the authorities actively aimed to stifle certain sorts of production)? In other words, was it an issue for the Ministry of Agriculture or the Ministry of Food? The implications of the failure to reach a conclusion on this problem were significant, as an unfortunate battle line was drawn between the commercial and the amateur grower. In a further spin off, the Diggers for Victory in the countryside were set against those from the town. In the end, a solution of sorts was found not within the corridors of Whitehall but through the good sense of the ladies of the Women's Institute.

In line with the Ministry of Agriculture's pre-war policy, at the start of the conflict Reginald Dorman-Smith had been reluctant to do anything that he considered might put the commercial sector's noses out of joint. What to do with excess produce was a source of contention for policy makers from the earliest days of the campaign, but Ministry minutes from January 1940 are indicative of where their loyalties lay:

> As it would be undesirable to encourage much direct marketing of vegetables as this would only be done at the expense of the small greengrocer, it appears that the cooperation of the retailer should be sought in framing any plan for the organisation of rural growers as is suggested.

Thus the issue was seemingly one to be dealt with at the distribution, as opposed to production, end and so theoretically became the responsibility of the Ministry of Food. Yet the same set of minutes also outlined a suggested solution that highlights the confusion within the Ministries themselves as to who should be responsible for what:

> In the Great War, the Food Production Department (which was then responsible for administering the food production campaign in England and Wales) developed a very active and popular movement for preserving at home the produce of allotments and gardens ... I am not sure whether, under present conditions, it would properly fall within the scope of the Ministry of Food or of the Agricultural Departments.

At the beginning of February 1940, disposal of excess produce was the subject of a parliamentary question by Colonel Charles Ponsonby. 'Is the Dig for Victory campaign,' he asked, 'designed to encourage the small private grower to cater for his own household requirements or is he to be encouraged to produce a surplus; and, in the latter case, how is he to dispose of it?' Dorman-Smith's answer, to all intents and purposes, was a fudge:

> The campaign is designed to encourage the small private grower to cater for his own household requirements. It is recognised, however, that the question of securing the effective use of surplus produce must be examined, and I am arranging, in consultation with my Right Honourable. friend the Minister of Food, for this to be done.

A few days later Dorman-Smith addressed the conference of the National Allotment Society, giving a clearer message that amateur producers were there to top up the offerings of the commercial producers but not to encroach on their markets. He told them:

> There will be no famine in fresh vegetables but the professional growers' very efficient production can with advantage be augmented on allotments and in private gardens. The new allotment drive does not aim at competing with the market gardening industry, which must be maintained for the national service. It is not intended that allotments should grow produce for sale.

Such a solution was fine for urban Diggers for Victory who were unlikely to produce anywhere near the volumes that might challenge the trade, but the situation for rural amateurs was rather different; with more space available and an ingrained tradition of agriculture and horticulture, the potential for high crop yields was clear. There was a growing sense that their particular circumstances were given less consideration than those of their city-dwelling compatriots. As Mr Middleton put it in December 1940: 'I have an uneasy feeling that in this campaign we are concentrating on the towns and neglecting the villages, where there is usually plenty of available land, abundant fresh air, and willing hands to do the work.'

It was a subject Middleton would return to often, particularly in his *Daily Express* column. Why should rural growers put in the effort to produce decent yields if anything not consumed by their immediate circle of family and friends was destined to go to waste? Referring to the plight of the village grower in September 1942, Middleton suggested the need for a different approach: 'He can grow vegetables and is inclined to be critical of well-meant technical advice. He is a little tired of prop-aganda; posters on a barn door portraying a boot and a spade fail to rouse his enthusiasm. What he needs is a direct inducement to grow more ... "Dig for Victory!" is an attractive slogan. May I suggest another one to go with it? "Food for the towns – money for the villages."'

In May 1940, the Ministry of Agriculture had found itself with a get-out clause when responsibility for the disposal of surplus crops from private gardens and allotments was formally handed over to Lord Woolton and the Ministry of Food. It undertook a programme of regular consultations with a variety of bodies including the Ministry of Agriculture, the National Federation of Women's Institutes and the National Allotment Society. In the summer of 1940, the decision was taken to set up a new group of sub-bodies to look afresh at the question at the local level, and so the County Garden Produce Committees were established.

Around this time, Woolton penned a missive to Hudson. Woolton was clear in his mind that if the nation was to have adequate supplies of the right foods to ensure an overall improvement in nutrition levels, whatever fresh vegetables could be produced needed to remain in the system. He outlined what he considered was a basic flaw with the campaign as it had been run up to that point. It was a thinly veiled slap on the wrist to Hudson personally:

… I gather that the allotment movement has to some extent been checked through consideration of the interests of commercial growers. If this is the case I cannot help feeling that a mistake has been made. The case for increasing consumption of fresh vegetables is so great that vested interests should not be allowed to restrict the Government effort … The policy should be the maximum production on allotments and private gardens and the distribution of surplus produce not required by the cultivator to families which need it.

An article in *The Times* on 26 September 1940 suggested an alternative market for surplus produce:

The experience of a wartime grower of fruit and vegetables on a large scale in Sussex may encourage others in like case to persevere, as she has done, in efforts to find a market for their produce. A solution to her problem was provided by the arrival in the neighbourhood of more troops, to whom she arranged to supply the large surplus for the production of which she had put under cultivation all the available land on her extensive estate.

However, the article made clear that this was but a partial solution, continuing:

> ... others who, like her, obeyed official exhortations to 'Dig for Victory' have not been so fortunate. They find their produce left on their hands, and some of them do not know where to turn for advice on the likeliest way to seek markets for it.

The problem rolled on into 1941. In March, Hudson was asked in Parliament, 'whether arrangements are being made for the collection of surplus vegetables, perishable and other, not only from established growers but from the innumerable small growers and allotment holders who have been stimulated by the 'Grow More Food' campaign and who are preparing to grow more vegetables than are necessary for their own households?'

The answer the Minister of Agriculture gave seemed now to suggest that the problem should be warded off by stemming production at source. He said:

> I have not encouraged the small grower and allotment holder to grow the maximum quantity of vegetables indiscriminately: such a policy would almost certainly lead to the production of a large unconsumable surplus of summer vegetables of the perishable type, and to disappointment and discouragement. The policy I advocate for the amateur grower is one of orderly cropping, with the cropping so planned that a succession of vegetables is obtained all year round, that overproduction of summer vegetables is avoided, and that any production surplus to the

grower's own requirements is of non-perishable vegetables which can be stored for use during the winter months.

That this was now the official policy clearly came as news to at least one chairman of a Garden Produce Committee. A certain Miss Talbot, who operated in Hertfordshire, was driven to write directly to the Ministry. Her letter paints a vivid picture of the problems caused at the local level by the lack of a cogent policy on this question. Indeed, one can feel the palpable panic in her tone as she confronts the spectre of social ostracism for the inconstancy of a government she has tried to serve to the best of her ability:

> If it is true that the Ministry of Agriculture has reversed its declared policy, i.e., that villages were to aim at being self-supporting, but that any surplus of root vegetables produced over and above their own requirements would be guaranteed at market, it will have the most devastating effect on the food production campaign. The villages will consider that they have been led on by false promises, and none of us who have passed on the Ministry of Food's assurances about marketing will ever be able to show our faces again.

Lord Woolton seems to have become frustrated by the contradictory messages too. The minutes of a meeting at the Ministry of Food on 13 February 1941 report him as saying, 'It was not good government if two departments were doing the same job,' and that he 'wanted to get that difficulty settled'. The notes of one of his civil servants dated March 1941 got to the very heart of the problem: 'It is also questionable whether the Minister would wish to associate himself with a policy of restricting food production in the interests of the market gardener, even if this, in fact, is the policy of the Ministry of Agriculture.'

Nonetheless, in March 1941 a memo was sent from the Ministry of Agriculture to the Federation of Women's Institutes explaining that the responsibility for the work of the County Garden Produce Committees was to revert back from the Ministry of Food to Hudson and his team. In July, Hudson said: 'As the Minister of Agriculture is responsible for production and the Minister of Food for distribution, the obvious good and administrative procedure was to put this matter under the Minister of Agriculture and not under the Minister of Food, because we hope, and I still believe it to be right, that the best way to deal with a surplus is to avoid it.'

As the issue ping-ponged between the two departments, the First Baron Davies questioned the Duke of Norfolk, who was Joint Parliamentary Secretary of the Ministry of Agriculture, in the House of Lords: 'In the first place, may I ask the noble Duke why it is that the partnership which apparently existed between the Ministry of Agriculture and the Ministry of Food has apparently now been dissolved?'

Then he posed his single most pertinent question: 'So I would again ask, what really is the policy of the Ministry? Is it to encourage or to discourage the growing of vegetables?' It was quite extraordinary that such a question should need to be asked of a spokesman for the Dig for Victory campaign, and yet it was entirely justified. Lord Norfolk responded thus:

It has now been decided that where there is a surplus amount of vegetables which it is possible to keep, and there are not the available storage facilities in the growing area, arrangements will be made for collecting and storing such surplus. But it is quite obvious that it would be impossible to collect all the perishable vegetables which might be produced as surplus production, because of difficulties connected with the supply of petrol and the available means of transport. To do so, it would be necessary to have transport vehicles going round the country continuously. In the case of vegetables which would keep, however, it does not much matter whether they are collected one week or the next. I hope that my noble friend will be satisfied with this explanation.

One suspects the noble friend, along with a great many others, was not. A *Times* editorial of 5 June 1942 reveals that the mini soap opera rumbled on:

At the present moment the public, after having been exhorted to 'dig for victory', are shocked to hear that hundreds of tons of fresh vegetables are allowed to rot or are ploughed back into the ground because the grower cannot obtain a remunerative price, or even sell them at any price, while high prices are being asked for them in the retail shops.

So the argument continued to go in circles, producing a rather curious situation. Woolton and the Ministry of Food, who might have been expected to baulk at the extra burden of establishing distribution channels for surplus produce, were in fact seemingly happy to take on the additional work; while the Ministry of Agriculture, responsible for increasing the country's food output, attempted to restrict the productivity of the keenest amateur gardeners.

It fell to the Women's Institute, under the guidance of its agricultural advisor Elizabeth Hess, to rise above the vested interests and political flannel, and implement a sensible, workable scheme for disposing of surplusses. As early as 1938, the WI Agricultural Sub-Committee had received a £500 grant from the Ministry of Agriculture towards its aim of encouraging 'production and the best use, preservation and marketing of home-grown produce'. In rural areas, the WI – along with the National Allotment Society, rural community councils and county horticultural organisers – worked towards making best estimates of the volume of vegetables in each county that would be available for market. Plans were then put in place to take these stocks to collection centres where they could be graded and, where suitable, redirected to the greengrocery trade, either directly to retailers or through wholesale markets. Local allotment societies were to carry out a similar role in urban areas, although the prospect of large-scale surpluses from the towns was remote. Where there was an urban excess, it was usual practice to find a home for it with the local hospital or another community institution.

There were similar regulations for dealing with fruit, though the quantities in question were on a much smaller scale. Maybe the WI's greatest achievement was the establishment of a network of over 5,800 Preservation Centres, geared up to preserve and distribute stores of perishable fruit and, to a lesser extent, vegetables. WI members became highly skilled operators of canning machines, many of which were donated by sister organisations in the USA and Canada, and the centres became filled with tins, bottles and Kilner jars ready for market or to be donated to worthy recipients, including hospitals and schools.

The minute books of the Carlton and Chellington WI, in Bedfordshire, provide an insight into just how much good work was being done. In November 1939, 88 lbs of potatoes were collected from members and sent to the county hospital (there were obviously skilled potato-growers within the ranks; in October 1940, Mrs Wykes won the branch competition for growing 16lb 13oz from a single spud). In May 1940, 153 eggs were sent to Dr Barnardo's homes, and a members' trading stall was set up to begin operating the following month, selling volumes of produce that were uneconomical for a commercial dealer but which otherwise would have gone to waste.

The National Federation wrote in July 1940 to request that any surplus fruit be turned into jam, and in September 1940, Carlton and Chellington reported: 'More than 2,000 lbs of various kinds of jam had already been made and the inspector who came to see it was very pleased and said that if we had any difficulty in selling the jam we could put it on the list for selling to London shopkeepers.' Bedfordshire as a whole had thirty-five preservation centres by the end of the year, which in 1940 alone used 9 tons of sugar in the production of 44,800 lbs of jam. The WI's *Produce Guild Guide and Handbook* of 1943 quoted the Earl of Portsmouth on the organisation's communal jam-making: 'It opens a vision of self-help, of returning skill, home craft, and cooperative work.'

A further glimpse of the astounding contribution made by the WI is provided by an interview broadcast on 8 February 1946 on *Modern Countryman*, a radio programme for the West of England Home Service. It was conducted with Mrs Dorothy Hebditch, a Somerset farmer's wife and the WI's 'Coordinator of Fruiting' (a venerable job title indeed) for Crewkerne and Ilminster districts:

Our homes were full to overflowing with evacuees, land girls and soldiers stationed in the village. Every moment seemed full up. Yet somehow when fruit came in we made time to deal with it – to make jam and chutney and so on … There wasn't much time to waste when you got a telephone call saying that someone had 12 lbs of plums they couldn't sell: 'Could we deal with them?' 'No,' you'd say, 'we can't manage that quantity – but Ilminster with its huge pans and its canner could.'

Imagine our faces when, after straining all our blackberries through sieves to make regulation jam, we heard in one of our village shops: 'I don't want none of that there WI jam. I do want something with pips in it.'

Each year over the period 1940–45, the WI membership in Somerset made enough jam to fill the annual ration entitlement of 4,100 people. 'Even if the men make fun of us sometimes, they always know where to turn when there's a job of work to be done,' Mrs Hebditch recalled with pride. There were other organisations too that played their part at various stages of the campaign, providing help with growing, preserving and distributing – among them the Scouting and Guiding movements, the Salvation Army and the Women's Voluntary Service (WVS). The latter, set up in 1938 on the suggestion of the Home Secretary, Sir Samuel Hoare, and led by the Dowager Marchioness of Reading, was envisaged as a means of giving women the opportunity to contribute to civil defence. Their work encompassed the provision of sustenance and welfare to the victims of aerial bombing. Among many other duties, the women ran mobile kitchens and communal feeding centres. In time they would also supply morale-building snacks to those who volunteered to help with bringing in the harvests. Seventy thousand pies were served up in the autumn 1941 Rural Pie Scheme alone. Additionally, the WVS ran a Food Leaders scheme, in which talks were given on cooking and maintaining good nutrition in a post-air-raid environment. Their work was often dangerous, and the WVS lost 241 members in the course of carrying out their duties during the war.

The efforts of the WI and these other voluntary bodies only served to make the hand-wringing of the political classes seem still sillier. The government's handling of the question of surplus produce would, in a different age, have provided wonderful material for an episode of the 1980s TV comedy *Yes Minister*. Dorman-Smith and then Hudson and their teams had, to a large extent, unnecessarily made a rod for their own back. Of course, it was important that no wartime government campaign should undermine the commercial food industry, which would be expected to go on working when peace resumed, but that was simply never on the cards. While Dig for Victory produced impressive results over the course of the war, overproduction was at worst sporadic and never posed a genuine threat to the livelihoods of commercial growers.

The split in the policy direction of the Ministries of Agriculture and Food on this issue was an unfortunate blip, which served only to infuriate and mystify those interested parties following the argument closely and perhaps held back the campaign from even greater achievements. Thankfully, though, most gardeners on the ground simply got on with the serious business of planting and nurturing, enjoying the results of their hard work and perhaps sharing any spare with their friends and neighbours. It is a salutary lesson for politicians in general – then and now – that luckily the general public don't listen too carefully to what they say.

As a footnote to the episode, a minute from a Ministry of Food meeting after the war, on 7 May 1946, neatly summarised the confusion: 'As you know, the division of function between ourselves and the Ministry of Agriculture has been a moot point ever since the Ministry of Food was created.'

10. Step on It!

By the time of Churchill's ascension to power in May 1940, the population as a whole was becoming better adapted to the conditions of wartime life, with vast numbers now psycho-logically ready to embrace the work demanded by Dig for Victory. The unresolved excess-produce issue aside, Hudson and Woolton oversaw a mass mobilisation of Diggers for Victory, running the campaign with creativity and pragmatism. What the two Ministries became so good at was refining and effectively delivering their messages. In the first place, they demystified the idea of 'growing your own' as well as simplifying administrative processes; this meant that a great many of those who might by instinct have been averse to taking on the task, became able to imagine themselves working the soil. The campaign also played on some of the fundamental desires and hopes shared by the general population – a wish to enjoy good food, to be able to keep their families fed, to have a leisure activity and a social outlet, to be able to say they had helped save shipping and, ultimately, played their part in defeating Hitler. One of the Ministry of Agriculture's adverts, entitled 'Step on it!', illustrates a typical motivational approach:

Dig Now – Don't Delay. Get your garden ready to grow your own vegetables – especially the kinds you can store. Apply to your local Council for an allotment and dig with all your might. Vegetables will be scarcer. Victory may well be won by the country with the most food. It is up to every man and woman to step on it now and make every garden a VICTORY GARDEN!

Such calls to action spectacularly won the hearts and minds of swathes of the population, and participation rates rocketed throughout the second half of 1940 and beyond. Where 230,000 had taken up shovels in anger by mid-April 1940, the figure had risen to 541,000 a year later. In December 1941, Churchill addressed the US Congress, stating that: '… our transformation from easy-going peace to total war efficiency has made very great progress'. A contributor to the Mass Observation project reported that same month that, '… practically every garden in Britain now produces vegetables, which lots of people with small gardens thought was rather a vulgar thing to do before, except on an allotment away from the house.'

Rob Hudson reported on the progress of the campaign on 18 March 1942 and was able to outline impressive achievements:

Allotment holders and private gardeners are producing between £10,000,000 [c. £275 million today] and £15,000,000 [c. £400 million today] worth of vegetables, thus relieving a corresponding amount of land on farms for the growing of other crops, which the private individual cannot grow. We are still making every effort. There are a few black spots, but we are making every effort to stir them up.

In his column for the *Daily Express* on 24 September 1942, Mr Middleton summed up the situation in his inimitable style:

> We can turn our gardens into munitions factories, for potatoes and other vegetables are munitions of war as surely as shells and bullets are ... Do not think of your allotment as an ordeal or a wartime sacrifice. Regard it as your pleasant and profitable recreation ... And what can be said of the campaign so far? We have shouted 'Dig for Victory!' from screen, platform and poster. Has it produced the expected results? Broadly speaking, I think so. The country is now definitely garden minded, but we still have a long way to go.

There had, indeed, been a fundamental change in behaviours. Official figures revealed that by 1942, out of all those families who formerly grew only flowers, only 20 per cent were now not growing vegetables. Nearly 40 per cent were devoting three-quarters or more of their garden space to vegetable cultivation. The years 1942–43 proved to be the peak of the Dig for Victory campaign. By that stage, the public were well adapted to the peculiar routines of wartime existence, understood fully the severity of the food position and were conscious that the future remained uncertain. That is to say, they were settled enough in the patterns of wartime life to throw themselves wholeheartedly into the campaign and, meanwhile, could draw on their fears of what lay ahead as a motivational tool.

In 1943, government estimates suggested the number of allotments was somewhere between 1.5 and 1.75 million. That, it now seems, was an overestimate but not outrageously so. In reality, the figure rose from around 835,000 in 1939 to

1,400,000 in 1943, an increase of almost 68 per cent. The area of land covered with allotments rose from 95,700 to 136,800 acres over the period, an increase of 43 per cent. It would also be fair to assume that, thanks to the campaign, those allotments were being more intensively cultivated by better-informed growers.

After the relaunch of Dig for Victory in February 1943, *The Times* attempted to calculate the effect of the campaign when private gardens were taken into consideration (their calculations were made on the basis of the government's marginal overestimation in plot numbers):

> ... there are now 1,750,000 allotments in the country. The standard size is 10 rods, which means that 16 plots run to an acre ... Probably in wartime the food plots in house gardens are twice as many as on the allotments ... The reckoning of 3,500,000 food plots apart from the allotments may be below the mark, and as there are the large gardens as well as the small, perhaps the 10-rod average can be allowed. If so it means that the spade has dug, for food cultivation, three times the area of Rutland or the Isle of Wight ... It is estimated that some 4,000,000 families now grow their own vegetables; and they are now advised, such is the plenty of the commoner vegetables, to concentrate on the lesser-known kinds, especially the green. Not that the full target has yet been reached: local ambition is asked to aim yet higher in 1943, and institutions like schools and hospitals are urged to make themselves self-supporting in vegetables.

But the story of the Dig for Victory campaign is not one best understood through statistics. It comes instead from the ordinary men, women and children who laboured in their gardens and allotment plots, creating its narrative with their sweat and toil. As the *Daily Express* put it on 7 August 1942:

> What really counts is the enthusiasm and effort of the gardener, the constant digging, hoeing, weeding, raking, thinning – the things which require labour and command interest. They induce in the gardener a feeling that he is working to a worthwhile end, making a valuable contribution in voluntary work towards winning the war.

Motivations for taking up the horticultural gauntlet were varied: for some, it was the chance to get out in the open, for others the opportunity to socialise, or to improve their diets and menus; but perhaps most important was the feeling that they were 'doing their bit'. Those available to become growers were by and large those not able to serve in the armed services – for reasons of age, gender, ill health or incapacity, or because they were required to remain at home for other essential war work. In short, growing fell to the people who might otherwise have felt that they were unable to contribute to the war effort as much as the sailors, soldiers and airmen on the front line. The Ministries of Food and Agriculture returned time and again to the theme of 'food as a munition of war', promoting the notion of growing as essential to the national effort. In 1942, Lord Woolton declared: 'Ever since I have been Minister of Food I have taken the pessimistic view of the food situation. If I hadn't you wouldn't be so well off now. The war may be long, and wise people prepare for the worse.'

Nor were there too many barriers to entry into the Dig for Victory army. Even those who lacked a garden of their own (or were languishing on a long waiting list for an allotment, as happened in many parts of the country) could get involved. The Ministry of Agriculture's Dig for Victory leaflet No. 24 suggested:

> Town dwellers who possess no garden and are unable to cultivate an allotment need not despair of being able to add to their food supplies through their own effort. Many houses and flats possess flat-leaded roofs, which provide an excellent opportunity for roof gardening; but when there is no roof of this type there are always window boxes that may be successfully used to grow certain crops.

While vegetable gardening may traditionally have been the preserve of the man of the house, the government was quick to recognise that if the Dig for Victory campaign was going to be successful, it was crucial to get children and, even more importantly, women on board. A series of posters issued in support of the campaign were designed specifically to attract them. One, a rather text-heavy example, appealed to the housewife's sense of responsibility for the well-being of her family:

> Women! Farmers can't grow all your vegetables. You must grow your own ... It's up to you to provide the vegetables that are vital to your children's health – especially in winter. Grow all you can. If you don't, they may go short. Turn your garden over to vegetables. Get the older children to help you. If you don't have a garden ask your local council for an allotment. DO IT NOW.

Another Dig for Victory ad, rather more blessed with brevity, used the slogan 'Start digging NOW – women and older children as well as men.' The appeal to the better nature of the women of the Home Front was a weapon wielded with great potency by Lord Woolton who, in a speech in 1941, emphasised the role women had to play in the war effort: 'It is good to think that posterity will learn from those who had to cater in Britain's front line. After all, housewives are war-workers same as anybody else, aren't they?' In September of that year, a broadcast on the BBC for the Ministry of Agriculture reiterated the message, although its attempts to persuade listeners that women were just as up to the job as men ended up sounding distinctly patronising: 'There are lots of fine *women* gardeners. Gardening is a job women can do well. It's not easy – but it's healthy. It's better anyhow than standing in queues ... Our future depends as much as food as on tanks and planes and ships.'

Patronising or not, the message was getting through and in June 1942, the country's first-recorded Women Allotment Holders' and Gardeners' Association was set up in Preston. That same year, Mrs Cope Morgan, the subject of a BBC Overseas African Service programme (*Calling Africa: Digging for Victory in a Convent Garden*), described how she got stuck into the campaign in a mostly male environment:

In our neighbourhood was a convent, with high surrounding walls and a large garden ... But the house was now deserted, there were bomb-craters in the flowerbeds, and the grounds had been acquired by the local Borough Council for wartime allotments. Listeners in Africa who think of ground space in terms of hundreds of acres, will smile when I explain that an average allotment is 30 x 90 FEET! We duly applied for one, paid our modest rental of 5s., were given a key to the garden and proceeded to inspect it. At first sight on a November afternoon, I must admit, our allotment was a depressing sight ... only a stretched piece of string divided us from our neighbours. There were about thirty allotment holders, a delightfully mixed bag: clerks, retired gardeners, a caretaker, salesmen, teachers, a bus driver, an ex-soldier (interned by the Germans during the last war and who was determined not to risk being hungry again), a police officer, daughter and myself. Of course, advice was showered on <u>us</u> – for we were the only WOMEN holders ... Whenever I thought it time to keep our end up, I could always do it with lurid stories of West Africa and white ants – no-one could compete with me there! ... We are now preparing for another gardener's year, full of hope that it will be even better than the last.

Joan Pennington, a schoolgirl at the time from the market town of Todmorden in the West Riding of Yorkshire and now a local WI president in Cambridgeshire, has her own memories of female ingenuity in the garden:

In the 1940s, when my dad was serving in the Royal Artillery in Europe, I was in an all-female home with my mum and her sister so we had to get on with jobs that a man might be expected to do and one of those was digging for victory to help with very real food shortages. So we set about clearing our bit of grass to plant spuds, the easiest thing we could grow! Mum dug and I 'helped' with weeding. The fun came with planting. Our neighbour, Mrs Parker, had lost a leg in an accident when young and used a crutch like a female Long John Silver. So after we'd dug, Mrs P. came with her crutch and planted it firmly into the soil, hopping round to make a hole into which went the spuds. The crop was great and gave us tasty new potatoes in due course. The whole planting process must have looked hilarious and we certainly enjoyed ourselves. Wartime women were very resourceful!

However, female uptake of allotments remained slightly disappointing. In August–September 1942, the Ministry of Agriculture undertook a survey into the effects of the Dig for Victory campaign, compiling the returns of 3,000 allotment holders. It had been hoped that of these, at least 250 would have been from women, but the report's authors were forced to concede that, 'Unfortunately it was not possible to find this number and in the end only 183 were seen.'

Many children were to play an active role in the campaign, helping out in the family garden or on the allotment plot. For some youngsters, allotment work became a staple of life, as much a fixture of the week as school, church on Sunday and trips to see Grandma. One child, a girl called Joyce Smith who lived in Croydon on the outskirts of London and was aged ten or eleven in 1940, kept a diary in which she detailed her regular contributions to her father's allotment. The entry for 31 December 1940 is a particularly poignant one, as she paints a picture in which the terror of German bombing and her work on the beloved allotment sit together as all part of normal life: 'Four hundred raids this year in London. Onion seeds and leek seeds planted.'

Children could also get involved through a variety of organisations, including Cubs, Scouts, Brownies and Girl Guides. Many of them spent long and happy days helping to pick wild fruits and other crops to be used medicinally, such as rosehips. Still more went on working holidays to farms, particularly at busy times such as harvest. However, the most common method of drawing children into the campaign was through school-based projects.

In *Voices from the Home Front*, Felicity Goodall quoted an essay written by one D. Madge in September 1940 concerning the allotments at the Kneller Boys School in Twickenham:

> Ever since war began the School's Field has been dug up into allotments 16 by 6 yards. All of them bear vegetables of some kind such as turnips, carrots, beetroot, cabbage, marrows, potatoes, Brussels sprouts etc. They are all worked by the boys themselves. The ground is very dry and the things aren't growing so well but the weather is breaking now and looking more like rain. Boys could come up to their allotments during the holidays, which owing to the war were only a fortnight. Just before the holidays a boy in the school stole most of the fruit from the orchard, but it was not long before he was found out. A lot of the vegetables are now being sold to the school and the money which we get is given to the Red Cross. Boys are still doing their bit 'Digging for Victory'!

It was inevitable that schools in rural locations were even more immediately geared towards this sort of work, being immersed in an agricultural environment and populated with pupils for whom the growing of crops and rearing of animals was a familiar enterprise. A particularly fine example was the Maisemore School Club, located just north of Gloucester. It ran a miniature farm that included pigs, poultry, rabbits and beehives. The children cultivated an area of garden covering almost a quarter of an acre, doing all aspects of the work themselves. They elected their own management committee and devised a comprehensive work rota, with pupils sacrificing their free time at weekends and during school holidays to ensure that all essential work was done. As of 1943, the farm could boast hugely impressive production figures – 8 tons of bacon, 50,000 eggs, 5 cwts of rabbit meat, 5 cwts of honey and vast amounts of vegetables of many types.

Margaret Brown, who was ten years old at the war's start, remembered how her own rural primary school embraced the Dig for Victory campaign from a very early stage. With the school's resident gardeners having been called up to serve in the armed forces, she and a group of her friends in the top class put themselves forward to cultivate the borders of the school garden, a job they became devoted to; they gave up their playtimes and evenings for the cause, and even their days off school (when the evacuees from London used the school for their own separate lessons).

By 1941, Margaret had moved on to the local girls' grammar school, which prided itself on an ethos that emphasised 'service to the community'. A school Dig for Victory corps was inaugurated in the early part of the war. Members wore a green armband, embroidered with crossed fork and spade, which resulted in their becoming known as the knife-and-fork brigade. They were taught basic techniques such as double digging (that is to say, digging one trench and then refilling it with the soil from the next trench) and began to help cultivate a corner of the school grounds, near the underground air-raid shelters and a static water tank. This garden was eventually able to supply a variety of produce including rhubarb, sprouts and celery to the school kitchen. A group of Italian prisoners of war were also employed in the school grounds during several phases of the war, although pupils were strictly kept away from them.

The corps instituted a programme to send parties of older pupils to a local farm that was suffering from a shortage of labour. All girls over thirteen qualified for the scheme, which involved providing a day's labour every month. Although Margaret had not yet reached the lower age limit, she was determined to play her part. So, driven by a burning sense of anger and injustice, she began a correspondence with the Ministry of Agriculture, complaining that younger children should not be prohibited from getting involved. She received an official acknowledgment of her letter but there was no further progress until she was called to see her headmistress shortly before her thirteenth birthday. The imposing matriarch of the school informed the girl that she would, after all, be allowed to join the scheme at least a little early. Though no mention was made of her communication with the Ministry, Margaret was convinced that the issue had indeed been brought to the attention of the school. She remembered the jubilation she felt on first joining the working party: 'A Ministry of Agriculture vehicle backed up to the front entrance of the school – unheard of – and I proudly walked down the front steps, normally out-of-bounds, and climbed with my packed lunch aboard the lorry.'

Not all children would have such happy memories though. Ivan James was a pupil at Newport High School and was working on its allotment after school one evening when he had to go back into the building to collect his satchel. Heavy soil clung to his shoes and he left muddy footprints as he marched down the corridor. The headmaster heard his footfall and came out of his office to see who was there. When the headmaster remonstrated about the muddy deposits in the freshly cleaned corridor, the young lad protested that he had been carrying out essential work. Alas, the headmaster did not take well to being spoken back to and ordered James to come to his office the next morning, when he was caned. 'At the time I felt very offended,' said Mr James, 'as I had been helping the war effort. I expect I am the only person in the country who was punished as a result of the "Dig for Victory" campaign!'

Another group who took the campaign to their hearts were servicemen stationed on British soil. Often finding themselves in out-of-the-way places and short of leave, growing produce was one way to combat the looming threat of boredom and ennui. In April 1942, *The Times* ran an article commending RAF stations for their work towards the campaign and congratulating them on the excellent results they had produced the previous summer. The prediction for summer 1942 was that a large number of aerodromes up and down the country would be fully self-supporting in vegetables.

The Americans, never ones to hold back, soon got in on the act too. John Steinbeck, the great American novelist, was in 1943 a war correspondent with the *New York Herald Tribune*. Much of his journalism from the period was later incorporated into the volume *Once There Was a War*, published in 1958. On 15 July 1943, he filed a report that included the following observations:

> On the edges of American airfields and between the barracks of troops in England it is no unusual thing to see complicated and carefully tended vegetable gardens. No one seems to know where the idea originated, but these gardens have been constantly increasing. It is fairly common now that a station furnished a good part of its own vegetables and all of its own salad greens ... Men who are homesick seem to take a mighty pleasure in working with the soil.

However, he also noted that attempts to grow popular American treats that were not indigenous to Britain or suitable to the climate – including sweetcorn, peppers, watermelons and cantaloupes – mostly ended in frustrating disappointment!

The nation's employers also made a significant contribution to the campaign, both in the provision of allotment plots that a good number of firms established on their grounds and also for offering encouragement (and on occasions, even a little time off) to workers keen to get involved. The government made several appeals to employers, such as this statement from November 1940:

> To Every Employer: The Minister of Agriculture, Mr. R.S. Hudson, appeals for cooperation. Employers can help me in my 1940/41 'Dig for Victory' Campaign ... May I appeal to you to encourage your staffs to take up allotments and to turn their gardens over to vegetable production ... every man and woman who can wield a spade has a part to play.

On 11 September 1942, the MP for Consett, David Adams, enquired of Hudson, 'whether he has yet made an appeal to industrial employers throughout the country to make available to employees, as allotments for their food production and also for works canteen requirements, suitable land adjoining their respective factories?' Hudson confirmed he would be doing so again before the launch of that year's campaign.

It was greatly to the benefit of Dig for Victory that Hudson and Woolton were *in situ* for so long to oversee its progress. Hudson remained till the war's end and then handed control into the more than capable hands of Tom Williams. By the time Woolton finished his stint at the Ministry of Food in 1943, before moving over to the Ministry of Reconstruction, much of the essential work towards establishing Dig for Victory was complete, and his successor, John Llewellin, simply had to keep up the momentum. Despite the odd hiccup in the government's execution of the campaign, this was a programme it believed in and one it was eventually able to persuade the people to believe in too. That is a rare achievement for any government at any time. In the words of Lord Woolton in 1942: 'The line of Food Defence runs through all our homes.' It was a virtually irresistible argument.

11. Propagation

Once it had got the wind in its sails, Dig for Victory became a truly modern multi-media campaign, making use of all the mass-media platforms available to it: radio, films, newspapers and magazines, books, posters, songs and public events. Crucially, it made full use of the power of celebrity to cajole and persuade a sometimes uncertain public, whether through Churchill, Hudson and Woolton in the political sphere or via the great broadcasting names of the day like Freddy Grisewood and, most importantly for the amateur grower, Mr Middleton. If the technology had then been available, you can be sure that this would have been a campaign you could have befriended on Facebook, followed religiously on Twitter and downloaded highlights of on YouTube.

Hudson and his department realised that the success of the campaign hinged on communicating what could be intimidating volumes of practical advice in as simple and non-threatening a way as possible. Their chief method of doing so was through the provision of official pamphlets and guides, though things had not get off to a confident start with the ill-starred 'Grow More Food' pamphlet published in the autumn of 1939.

However, the pamphlet series was relaunched in 1941, devoid of basic errors and now rebranded under the 'Dig for Victory' banner – complete with the famous foot-on-spade image. By 1942, over 10 million of the leaflets were in circulation. Another triumph was *Garden Plot to Kitchen Pot*, a small booklet that included gardening tips from the Ministry of Agriculture and food tips from the Ministry of Food.

A total of twenty-six Ministry of Agriculture Dig for Victory pamphlets were published, which attempted to cover virtually every major question the new wave of growers might ask, whether tending a large allotment plot or the smallest window box. From the basics of digging to the intricacies of fruit and vegetable preservation, the pamphlets formed a comprehensive guide that served as a veritable horticultural encyclopedia for a generation. There are gardeners still active today who refer to the publications as their principle source of reference. Below they are detailed in the order in which they appeared:

1. Grow for Winter as well as Summer – Guide to All-Year-Round Planting
2. Onions/Leeks/Shallots/Garlic – Great for Winter
3. Storing Vegetables for Winter Use
4. Peas and Beans
5. Cabbages and Related Crops
6. How to Grow Root Vegetables for Winter
7. Manure from Garden Rubbish
8. Tomato Growing
9. How to Make Bordeaux and Burgundy Mixture in Small Quantities
10. Jam and Jelly Making
11. Bottling Fruit and Vegetables

12. Seed Potatoes

13. Storing Potatoes

14. Drying, Salting, Pickles, Chutneys

15. Potato Growing in Allotments and Gardens

16. Pests and How to Deal with Them

17. Potato Blight

18. Better Fruit – Disease Control in Private Gardens

19. How to Sow Seeds

20. How to Dig

21. Sowing Your Own Seed

22. How to Grow Small Fruits

23. Cropping Plan (5-Rod Plot)

24. Roof and Window-box Gardening

25. How to Prune Fruit Trees and Bushes

26. How to Use Cloches

The Ministry, however, did not rely on the written word alone, and also looked to deliver its message face-to-face. This was achieved most effectively through Dig for Victory events, including talks, demonstrations, shows and festivals that could last up to a week. They were an excellent way to foster relations between the government, local organising bodies and the public. An impressive roll-call of experts and popular personalities were persuaded to attend these occasions, while growers had a chance to socialise, learn and, of course, show off. Among those signed up by the government to spread the word was Godfrey Baseley, a former butcher who had carved out a career at the BBC in the 1930s. When his contract there was not renewed, he entered the civil service and throughout the first half of the war could be seen travelling around the Midlands in a van with a loudspeaker, offering advice on how to grow. He resumed his career at the BBC in 1943 and in 1950, no doubt influenced by his horticultural and agricultural experiences, devised a new radio drama called *The Archers* (now the world's longest-running soap opera).

A selection of the questions and answers from meetings in support of Dig for Victory were published in a booklet called *Gardeners Are Asking* ..., which described itself as a 'fount of Information on Home Food Growing'. They give a taste of the many and varied posers that growers faced:

How can I stop cats roaming over my allotment?

With garden pepper dust – or catapult!

****

Will the Ministry of Agriculture buy our surplus vegetables?

I don't know, but doubt it very much and don't see why they should. How about giving away the surplus to someone who hasn't a garden?

****

An incendiary bomb fell through the roof of my shed and vegetables stored there are now covered with fine grey powder. Will they be fit to eat?

If you wash the vegetables very thoroughly they should be alright, but there is no experience to guide us on this point.

Dig for Victory events often involved the awarding of prizes to growers (typically consisting of gardening supplies, small cash sums or War Savings Certificates). Growers could also qualify for Ministry of Agriculture Certificates of Commendation from August 1940. They became much-prized possessions, being reserved for those 'who cultivated a plot of land to the best advantage and so made a valuable contribution towards the Nation's effort to grow more food in time of war'. In October 1940, Hudson championed another scheme, providing patriotic householders with a sign to hang on their gates, reading 'This is a Victory Garden.'

A Ministry of Agriculture inquiry into the effects of the Dig for Victory campaign from August and September 1942 revealed that the Ministry's efforts had real impact. Fifteen per cent of post-1939 allotment holders attributed their taking of an allotment directly to the publicity drive, and 34.4 per cent recalled having seen specific Dig for Victory posters (a respectable figure considering that, as modern advertisers know so well, we often see and absorb information from advertising hoardings without consciously realising it). Forty-four per cent had obtained Dig for Victory leaflets, and of those who had received publicity, about a fifth had made the effort to note down particular pieces of advice that caught their eye. An impressive 27 per cent had visited a demonstration plot and, perhaps most tellingly of all, a whopping 91 per cent said they had no difficulty in getting advice, an irrefutable triumph for the Ministry.

Meanwhile, the Ministry of Food undertook other publicity campaigns that did not come under the Dig for Victory banner but which were vital in bolstering support for it. Among its most important contributions was to educate people in preparing produce so that eating it was a pleasure and not a chore – not that everyone necessarily appreciated their work in this area, though. R.J. Hammond wrote in his landmark study *Food*:

Gastronomically speaking, nothing could be more pathetic than the efforts of the Ministry of Food to devise, out of potatoes, dried egg, salt cod and the like, 'Victory Dishes' whose delights were extolled in terms to make a commercial advertiser blush. The monotony of British wartime diet was partly due to the retention of the form of pre-war dishes without their substance, much as a food crank will eat 'nut roasts' or drink 'dandelion coffee'.

This was to overstate the case, however. There were certainly some curious creations (anyone for 'murkey' – mutton formed into mock turkey – or Firefighter's Pie, Skinflint Pudding, and Tripe and no onions?). In addition, publications such as *How to Use Stale Crusts* seemed hardly designed to inspire, but other recipes represented the triumph of creativity in the face of adversity. On the front line were the food advisors, such as Marguerite Patten, who joined the Ministry in 1942 and a year later found herself in charge of the Food Advice Bureau at Harrods. She remembers:

> We didn't wait for people to come to us. We went out to find people. I started quite early on in my career with the Ministry on a stall in Cambridge market, showing people. We also went into canteens to talk to people over their lunchtimes – I don't think we were very popular interfering with lunch! We went to hospital outpatients units, into allotments and parks. Anywhere where there were people to talk to. I think the attitude of the Ministry was really very clever. They didn't dictate but they tempted people, lured them, talked to them as if they understood their problems. 'Do you want to hold a children's party? Let us help you.' 'Entertaining friends? Well, here's a

splendid menu you could make.' The attitude was to be helpful as possible. The man to praise for that was Lord Woolton. He was not only a wonderful manager but he also had this gift of communication. He was a cross between Father Christmas and your favourite uncle.

That said, tact was not always the watchword of the Ministry's officials. We might wonder what Miss Patten made of the words of the Parliamentary Undersecretary William Mabane, delivered in 1942 with a flamboyant disregard for gender equality: 'Fundamentally, men are better cooks than women, but this is no reason why some women should cook as badly as they do. Many people in this country have never really tasted vegetables. All they know is the sodden pap produced by over-boiling unprotesting vegetables in a bath of water.'

Perhaps the most famous and popular dish to emerge, and one that has stood the test of time, was Woolton Pie, named as a tribute to the Minister of Food. The Ministry was happy to promote the tasty dish, which was reputedly the invention of the head chef at the Savoy. The classic recipe required: 1 lb each of diced potatoes, cauliflower, swedes and carrots; 3 or 4 spring onions; 1 teaspoonful of vegetable extract; and 1 teaspoonful of oatmeal. The method went as follows: 'Cook all together for ten minutes with just enough water to cover. Stir occasionally to prevent the mixture from sticking. Allow to cool, put into a pie dish, sprinkle with chopped parsley and cover with a crust of potatoes or wholemeal pastry. Bake in a moderate oven until the pastry is nicely brown and serve hot with brown gravy.'

Some Ministry of Food campaigns were directly responsive to the specific requirements of the Dig for Victory drive at any given moment. Never was this more successful than when 'Potato Pete' and 'Dr Carrot' were unleashed on the world to encourage the consumption of those particular vegetables during gluts. These were the types of vegetables championed among Diggers for Victory because they were relatively easy to grow, offered a proud harvest and could be easily stored. Potatoes, for instance, could be kept either in sacks or clamps (an outdoor facility constructed from soil and straw). It was important, however, for the ongoing good of the campaign that produce was consumed relatively quickly and not left to fester.

The jovial Potato Pete burst on to the scene in 1940 to front the 'Eat More Potatoes' campaign, armed with a barrage of slogans: 'Potatoes keep you fighting fit!', 'Potatoes are part of the battle!' and 'Step lively with me.' He even had his own anthem, sung by the music-hall star Betty Driver, an actress destined to spend over four decades playing the character of Betty, the erstwhile barmaid of the Rovers Return in the ITV soap *Coronation Street* (whose famous hotpot would surely have won the approval of Lord Woolton). The song went:

> Here's the man who ploughs the fields.
> Here's the girl who lifts up the yield.
> Here's the man who deals with the clamp,
> So that millions of jaws can chew and champ.
> That's the story and here's the star,
> Potato Pete
> Eat up,
> Ta ta.

Another ditty also extolled the nutritional value of the spud:

There was an old woman who lived in a shoe.
She had so many children, she didn't know what to do.
She gave them potatoes instead of some bread,
And the children were happy and very well fed.

The campaign was a rip-roaring success and by the end of the war, potato consumption was up 60 per cent on pre-war levels.

The use of cartoon characters to promote vegetable consumption had enjoyed a strong recent history. In 1930s America, E.C. Segar's cartoon creation, *Popeye*, with his refrain 'I'm strong to the finish 'cause I eats me spinach!' was credited with raising the popularity of that particular vegetable. The Ministry of Food came up with Dr Carrot in the early days of the war, and he more than proved his worth, not least in 1942 when there was a 100,000-ton carrot surplus. Many carrots were sold at half price to be used in animal feed (and sprayed purple to ensure their correct usage!) but it was far more desirable that the human population took its fill. They were encouraged to this end by the dapper doctor, who carried a top hat, cane and suitcase, urging 'Let Dr Carrot protect you.'

In 1941, Hank Porter, an American artist working in the studios of Walt Disney, was employed by the Ministry to design an entire carrot family. This initially featured another Dr Carrot, but the home-grown one was not to be displaced, so in the end Porter came up with Carroty George, Clara Carrot and Pop Carrot. They featured in a series of cartoons and informative publications during 1941 and 1942 but never quite equalled the impact of the good doctor.

Dr Carrot's greatest campaign revolved around the slogan: 'Carrots keep you healthy and help you see in the blackout.' At the time, the Air Ministry was keen to promote the idea that carrots improved eyesight as an explanation for the recent upsurge in the success of RAF pilots bringing down German night bombers. They were, the public was told, simply eating more carrots and so could find the enemy more easily in the night sky. In fact, it was but a cover story to divert attention away from the Air Force's successful adoption of the Airborne Interception Radar system. Herbert Morrison, the wartime Minister of Supply, wrote in his 1960 autobiography that the scheme was 'typical of Ministry of Food ingenuity'.

Today the Dig for Victory campaign lives on most vividly in the striking posters that have come down to us. The artwork produced to promote the campaign was remarkably varied. The classic image remains the black and white photo of a boot on a shovel as it slices into the ground. In her BBC Overseas African Service broadcast on 11 March 1942 about her convent allotment, Mrs Cope Morgan explained the power it had to inspire her:

> It was the posters that did it – 'Dig for Victory!' Just working in an office (however much good work there was to do) and one's occasional fire-watching didn't seem enough; there was still some time to spare during the weekends, that sacred institution so beloved of Englishmen! Also, that poster was a challenge. The very large boot pressing in the spade was undoubtedly a man's – daughter and I felt quite able to prove that two pairs of smaller feet could do the job equally well.

The 'boot on the spade' poster, which first appeared in 1941 and was reproduced some four million times up to 1945, could hardly be accused of subtlety yet there is perhaps no more famous advertising image produced by any British government, with the honourable exception of the First World War poster *Your Country Needs You* featuring Lord Kitchener. The Dig for Victory poster is also at the centre of an intriguing mystery: exactly whose left foot is it in that boot? There are two major claimants to the title, both backed by contemporary sources.

The most widely touted owner of the said extremity (whose champions include the Imperial War Museum) was one Mr W.H. (William Henry) McKie, a senior member of the Acton Gardening Association and an allotment holder in Acton Vale. He was the subject of a story in the *Acton Gazette* on 7 February 1941, under the headline 'The Man whose foot all the nation knows.' With a long interest in horticulture, Mr McKie had originally come upon the joys of vegetable growing at the start of the First World War. However, like Mr Middleton, his real love remained with flowers and he was particularly renowned among his fellow Acton gardeners for his spectacular gladioli, dahlias and zinnias, all of which had won numerous competition awards over the years. Sixty-six years of age at the outbreak of the Second World War, he had listened to the call of civic duty and reverted to nurturing vegetables. Often to be found working away on his plot on both Saturdays and Sundays, he was there one day when official photographers came to the site and, so it was said, took the famous shot.

This tale is perfectly credible and was something of a propaganda coup – the story of an elderly gentleman at the heart of the community doing the right thing and making his contribution to the national effort, just as he had done in the Great War. The story of the rival claimant, Thomas Morgan Jones, may initially lack some of that romanticism but its leading protagonist lived out a remarkable war story of his own.

Tom Jones, a resident of Sunbury-on-Thames in Surrey, was

an artist with the Morgan-Wells advertising firm based at 9 Bishops Court, Chancery Lane in London. Six feet tall and of slender build, he had wanted to join the RAF but was turned down and so became eager to 'do his bit' in some other way. On 25 February 1941, less than three weeks after the Mr McKie story in the *Acton Gazette*, the *Daily Express* reported that Jones had broken his foot in an accident as he descended the steps of Westminster Bridge while on his war duties. To the *Daily Express*, there seemed no doubt that this was the man whose foot adorned the nation's billboards. 'DIG-FOR-VICTORY FOOT CAN DIG NO MORE' ran the headline above the story describing Jones as an enthusiastic gardener now only able to look on as his wife and children took care of the family vegetable plot.

Jones also detailed his version of the birth of the boot image:

One day about a year ago Mr Charles Wells, principal of the studio at which I worked, asked me to do a drawing for a photograph symbolising the national effort. I did a rough drawing in my lunch hour. That sketch formed the basis of the poster. We brought some soil from London's Lincoln's Inn Fields into the studio. I brought along my gardening boots and a pair of tweed trousers from home. The photograph, although set against a skyscape, was actually taken in the studio. The soil was spread on a board. I directed the lighting for the picture and it was photographed by Mr John Gill.

Gill apparently used a 35mm camera and the sky background was added later by technical darkroom wizardry. This version of the poster's genesis has been retold and substantiated several times over the ensuing decades – including in the *Guardian* in the 1970s, when a junior at Morgan-Wells described witnessing the shoot at first hand. Roy Jones, Tom's son, was a twelve-year-old when he was named in the *Express* piece; he corroborated the story in 2010 and said that the spade used in the picture had resided in his father's garden in Sudbury for many years after the war.

Tom Jones's own wartime experiences only got more interesting following his unlikely brush with fame. After leaving his advertising agency, he served with the Special Operations Executive and was based at Station XIV at Briggens, near Roydon in Essex. There he forged documents for agents operating in occupied Europe. He also claimed to have landed in a midget submarine in Normandy shortly before the D-Day landings to sketch the defences the Allies would face.

Ultimately, it must fall to the individual to decide which story about the poster they wish to believe but regardless, it remains a potent image and, at the time of writing, was enjoying a new wave of popularity – decorating a range of t-shirts, mugs and other merchandise.

There were many other posters that were similarly impactful, created by a disparate group of painters, illustrators and cartoonists. What united virtually all of the images was their boldness and simplicity, not only reflecting the many and various artistic styles of the first half of the twentieth century but also the paradoxical unshackling of the artistic spirit that war has regularly engendered throughout history.

The Ministry of Information built up a magnificent register of artists to call upon, including big names such as Henry Moore and Edward Ardizzone. Another, Dame Laura Knight, had become the first woman to be made a full member of Royal Academy in 1936. When the Ministry approached her at the war's start, she agreed to contribute her skills and produced some of the most distinctive work for the 'Lend a Hand on the Land' campaign (though her depiction of 'Ruby Loftus', the archetypal female munitions worker, was perhaps her most famous work of the period). Meanwhile, Milner Gray, who had been key to the foundation of the Society of Industrial Artists in 1930, was in 1940 named as head of the Ministry's Exhibitions Branch, which went on to produce a great deal of work for the Dig for Victory campaign.

John Gilroy was the man responsible for the *We Want Your Kitchen Waste* poster featuring an exceptionally gleeful-looking pig. Born in Newcastle-upon-Tyne in 1898, his career as a graphic and portrait artist took off after he won a scholarship to the Royal College of Art in 1919. In the 1930s, he was much in demand by advertisers, with his work for Guinness winning widespread praise. Apart from the Dig for Victory campaign, he also produced posters promoting the 'Careless Talk Costs Lives' and 'Make-Do and Mend' campaigns.

Abram Games, a largely self-taught modernist, was another highly successful commercial artist during the 1930s, his client list including Shell, London Transport and the General Post Office. Having joined the infantry in 1940, in 1942 he became the official War Office poster designer. He believed his time spent among ordinary soldiers made him better able to produce posters that spoke directly to them. The Ministry of Information adapted several of his designs for their own use, including one advising 'Grow Your Own Food.'

Still other campaign artists had intriguing back stories. Take, for instance, Eileen Evans, responsible for, amongst others, a poster entitled *Lend a Hand with the Potato Harvest*. She had joined the Ministry of Information's photographic division as a filing clerk in 1940, but her artistic gift was soon noticed and she was promoted to working in the design studio under the boss, Reginald Mount.

Another artist, Frederic Henri Kay Henrion, had been born in Nuremberg in 1914, before moving as a young man first to Paris and then to England, where he was one of an influential alliance of German-born designers. When war broke out he was interned but eventually found work with the Ministry, where his strong photomontage images were used to promote Dig for Victory.

Hans Schleger (known professionally as Zero) was also born in Germany, of Jewish heritage. He had left for New York in the 1920s, where he put his talents profitably to work in advertising. He returned to the land of his birth after the Wall Street Crash but decided to escape the growing anti-Jewish sentiment in Germany in 1932, when he came to Britain. He undertook projects for the likes of Shell and London Transport (for whom he worked on the iconic bus-stop sign) and was awarded British citizenship in 1939. His mother remained in Berlin and was transported to the Theresienstadt concentration camp in Czechoslovakia, then later to the Minsk ghetto. Yet for all the heartache he suffered, Zero's work (such as his effort entitled 'Rabbits can be fed on ...') remained jolly and upbeat – ideal for the Dig for Victory audience.

One of the most enduringly popular of the campaign's images is the painting by Peter Fraser of a smiling, pipe-smoking allotment holder, a fork on his shoulder, a basket of gorgeously fresh produce in his left hand and a bunch of carrots in the crook of his right arm. The slogan ran 'Dig on for Victory.' Fraser had been born on the Shetland Islands in 1888 but moved to the southeast of England and first had his work published in

Punch in 1912, the start of a long career working for magazines. After serving in the First World War, he started to have his own children's books published, with titles like *Funny Animals*, *Tufty Tales* and *Higgledy Piggledy Tales*. He had also illustrated the texts of a great many other writers by the time of the Second World War.

Perhaps just as popular was the rather sentimental depiction of a child with his (or perhaps her) back to us, carrying an oversized hoe and dragging a spade. It was adapted from a design by Mary Tunbridge which won a Ministry of Information competition open to members of the public. She is a woman of whom we know virtually nothing, except that she went on to produce other commercially successful work. She is not alone in being lost to history, though. A number of other artists responsible for several memorable images are now all but unknown – Le Bon, Paul Falconer and Xenia to name but a few.

12. Mr Middleton and Friends

While we may still regularly see many of these iconic images of the campaign, the vagaries of both wartime and the early BBC means that only a tiny proportion of wartime broadcasts were recorded and remain for us to listen to today. Yet radio was *the* medium of the war – available to the vast majority of the population and the natural home to the biggest stars of the day. Unlike now, when the country might converge as one for the odd event such as a royal wedding or funeral, or a particularly significant sports match, the wireless listeners of the 1930s and 1940s had scant choice in what they could listen to. So everyone but everyone was familiar with voices such as those of the comedian Tommy Handley, Mr Middleton, the Radio Doctor and broadcaster Freddy Grisewood, as well as the comic antics of the fictional Buggins family. All these, and assorted others, played a crucial role in embedding Dig for Victory into the national psyche.

In 1939, there were some nine million homes with BBC licences, covering about three-quarters of the country. In the six years of the war the Corporation broadcast something approaching two thousand food-related programmes. A 1942 survey into the Dig for Victory campaign revealed that 72 per cent of respondents who had a wireless set listened to gardening talks, with 36 per cent of those acting upon the advice offered – figures that modern broadcasting executives would probably kill for. Of the horticultural programmes available, Mr Middleton's *In Your Garden* dwarfed its competitors in popularity: 79 per cent of those who said they listened to gardening shows mentioned it by name; the next most popular show came up in only 13 per cent of responses.

The government made full use of the medium too. The annual relaunch of the campaign was marked by a ministerial address on the wireless, outlining the hopes and aims for the year ahead. Churchill also spoke on its behalf. In 1941, he made a speech primarily aimed at spurring on the nation's farmers but which had a message for the amateur grower too:

> The situation demands from each one of us still greater effort, still greater sacrifices, than we have yet made. Ships that would have brought food to our shores must now be used to meet the urgent needs of ourselves and our Russian allies for aeroplanes and tanks. You can release more ships by growing still more food in this country and so hasten the day of victory.

But above all others, Mr Middleton was the voice of Dig for Victory. On *In Your Garden,* his thoughtful, kindly delivery – rendered even more endearing by the odd dropped aitch – was the vehicle for many wise and memorable words, such as: 'An allotment is like the army. The first month is the worst: after that you begin to enjoy it.' Other pearls of wisdom included: 'Sweep your lawn before the first mowing,' 'Keep your tools clean,' and 'There is no substitute for digging, or if there is I haven't found it.'

Whether the BBC ever fully understood just what a diamond they had is not clear. A certain amount of damning with faint praise by his paymasters went on. When there was a slight falling off in his audience figures in the early months of 1940, the Corporation concluded it was because 'gardening is no longer a hobby and therefore his soporific appeal has diminished'. The more likely truth was that with the country at war, listening habits were simply adapting. A good number of Middleton's core audience were, in all likelihood, spending Sunday afternoons tending their vegetable patches as the government wanted them to, rather than staying at home with an ear glued to the wireless. According to an internal memo, there was, ultimately, an acknowledgement among the BBC management that '... Middleton's scripts are maintaining their high standard, and that the heavy fall in his audience figures is probably due to war conditions affecting the normal gardening fans,' as well as an admission that, 'We all think there is nobody who could fill his place adequately ...'.

Yet there were plenty of examples of his rather harsh treatment by the BBC. Paid twelve guineas per show, when Middleton came down with a nasty case of bronchitis and was unable to broadcast for several programmes running, his fee was dropped to nine guineas despite the fact that he prepared all the scripts as normal, with a staffer reading them out on air. On another occasion, he felt the wrath of both the BBC and the Ministry of Information for an unguarded but good-humoured comment he made during a discussion of the challenges of growing carnations while lime was in short supply: 'But cheer up,' he said, 'the way things are going at the moment there will soon be plenty of mortar rubble about.'

Conduct towards him hit a new low after the Middleton

family home fell victim to German bombing in the autumn of 1940, rendering the house uninhabitable until February of 1942. Mr Middleton went to stay with relations in Weston, Towcester, back in his native Northamptonshire. He applied to the BBC for extra petrol ration coupons to compensate for the additional travel he would need to undertake but it was rejected out of hand, with the BBC's attached memo revealing that they considered him 'grabbing' for having even suggested the idea. Their condescending attitude was summed up when they refused to clear him for an appearance on *The Brains Trust* radio show, decreeing that, 'Middleton's whole charm is that he is an amateur expert'. His ability to connect with people possessing all levels of knowledge was to his credit but his talents extended rather further than the BBC was giving him credit for.

Not that Mr Middleton's exploits were restricted to the radio. His abilities as a public speaker were in much demand for talks around the country and he was top of the list of any organisation seeking a judge for their Dig for Victory show. This was an area of his job he embraced warmly, trekking up and down the country uncomplainingly, his appearances drawing crowds as large as three thousand. His description of one local show as, 'complete with flags, jangles and wangles, a band, a few speeches, darts competitions, bowling for a pig and other sideshows,' illustrates not only a fine way with words but a genuine affection too. 'There is something extremely satisfying about winning a prize at a show,' he wrote. Nor did he attempt to hide his fundamental preference for flowers over vegetables: '... even a wartime Dig for Victory show is a poor affair without its flowers'. A colleague at the *Daily Express* wrote of him: 'It was not that he hated vegetables but rather that he found them dull. He could not love an onion where a dahlia might grow.'

Middleton's weekly gardening column for the *Express* had a circulation approaching seven million. He never shied from throwing himself into a pertinent debate or reprimanding a correspondent where he thought it was warranted. He began his column of 17 January 1942 by detailing a letter he had been sent: 'You tell me to dig up my lawn and grow food, the government shouts "Dig for Victory", but why should I, if it is only to put fat profits into the pockets of seed merchants? Do you think I am a perfect fool?' Middleton's considered response was, 'Well no, I wouldn't go as far as that but I do think it is rather foolish to write such piffle without a little knowledge.'

He published several guides both before the war and during, in support of the Dig for Victory Campaign. His last work was an encyclopaedia of gardening. He also worked for Boots as a horticultural consultant, the company's adverts reassuring the public that 'Mr Middleton approves all gardening products made by Boots the Chemists – The Gardener's Chemists.' However, Sunday afternoons presenting *In Your Garden* on the wireless was always his spiritual home.

After *In Your Garden*, the next greatest growers' show was *The Radio Allotment*, which ran from February 1941 until the end of the war and was described by the Ministry of Agriculture as 'an excellent feature'. It was a show of ten minutes (later lengthened to fifteen), offering practical advice from a genuine plot situated in Park Crescent, close to Broadcasting House in London.

Its original anchor was Roy Hay, a career horticulturist born in 1910 in Linlithgow. After a stint working for a seed merchant, he took over as Assistant Editor at the *Gardener's Chronicle* in 1936. In 1939, he moved to the Royal Horticultural Society to head up their publishing division and also began working on the Dig for Victory campaign at the Ministry of Agriculture. A man keen to do his duty, he was in addition a War Reserve Police Constable attached to the police station in Hyde Park.

According to a BBC Listener Research Report, *The Radio Allotment* (along with *In Your Garden*) appealed 'more to the novice than the experienced gardener'. Hay shared presenting responsibilities with several co-hosts including Michael Standing, Diana Hay, Raymond Glendenning, Sheilagh Millar, Stewart McPherson and Wynford Vaughan Thomas. In 1942, Hay left the show when he was transferred to Malta to oversee the food production programme there (and after the war he would serve as controller of the horticulture and seeds division of the British Zone in Germany). His role on the show was taken over by his father, Tom, a former Superintendent of the Royal Parks. This change was not altogether successful, though. A 1943 Listener Research Report revealed complaints that Tom Hay's Scottish brogue sounded 'old, indistinct, or disagreeable' while one listener noted that he 'just seems to walk around saying "Very good, yes, very good."' In 1944, Hay Snr received a rather strained letter from the Director of Outside Broadcasting, warning that the show was 'covering much of the same ground for the third year running'. It had doubtless run out of legs by the time it finished, but had served an important function even so.

Other notable gardening-based programmes included *Weekend Gardening*, *Back to the Land* and *Over the Border*, which involved discussions between panels in Edinburgh and London. The BBC began its Forces Programme in January 1940 and by the end of the year *Gardening for the Forces* was broadcasting to the troops. More popular still was *Ack Ack Beer Beer*, a programme produced by Bill MacLurg for men on anti-aircraft and balloon barrage sites, which included regular gardening talks for servicemen working their own allotments. There was also *The Practice and Science of Gardening*, a series devised with children in mind.

Fred Streeter (a farm worker's son from Sussex who had left school to become a farm labourer in the early 1890s when he was only twelve) had first appeared on the radio as a guest of Mr Middleton in 1935, by which time Streeter had risen to the role of head gardener at Petworth House. Blessed with a light touch and contagious enthusiasm, he was an immediate hit, and during the war became a regular on *In Your Garden* on the wireless and on the Dig for Victory circuit, discussing all subjects fruit-and-veg related. Indeed, after Middleton's death he would become the Corporation's main gardening man.

Another presenter particularly popular on the Dig for Victory show circuit was Donald McCullough, a high-profile writer and broadcaster of the day, particularly revered for his role as the question master on *The Brains Trust*, to which some 30 per cent of the population listened. In May 1942, he began presenting *Country Magazine*, a fortnightly programme aimed specifically at the rural population. In his 'spare time' he was a Public Relations Officer at the Ministry of Information.

Equally as important as the shows offering advice to those working in the garden or at the allotment were the programmes that focussed on the kitchen and offered ideas for the preparation and cooking of food. If Dig for Victory was to succeed, produce needed to be transported not only from soil to kitchen table, but carry on into the pot, to a plate and into tempted mouths. *Health in Wartime* and *The Kitchen in Wartime* both commanded steady audiences, but by far the most popular of this type of show was *The Kitchen Front*, which ran from 13 June

1940. That first episode included tips on planting vegetables, and was presented by S.P.B. Mais, a prolific author and journalist of the time who had broadcast the first *Letter from America* in 1933 but had no discernible background in food.

Broadcasting at quarter past eight in the morning, six days a week, the programme filled five minutes after the news bulletin and could bring in an audience of five million and more (some 15 per cent of the available audience). On offer, and delivered with great humour, were handy tips that the average housewife (the target audience) could pick up and use at once (ideally while out shopping that very day). A typical episode might begin with the presenter telling the audience: 'I'm here to save you money, to save you time, to save you trouble, to tell you of food that there's plenty of and of food that you've got to slow on.'

The show was an immediate hit, generating thousands of letters from captivated listeners in its first week. Within a fortnight it had received 30,000 requests for copies of the featured recipes. The Ministry of Food had a big hand in devising the content, with a team trying out all the recipes at a Ministry kitchen in Portman Square. Among the ministerial staff who worked on the scripts was Eileen Blair, the wife of George Orwell (whose real name was Eric Blair). While there were occasional skirmishes between staff from the BBC and those at the Ministry, relations were largely cordial during the life of the programme.

Information was presented by a variety of guests on *The Kitchen Front* but three of its great stalwarts were Freddy Grisewood, Ambrose Heath and Mabel Constanduros. Grisewood, known affectionately as 'Ricepud', was a smooth and appealing host. Born in 1888 the son of a rector in Worcestershire, he went to

University at Oxford and served in the First World War, suffering injuries from which he took several years to recover. He succeeded in carving out a career as a singer before joining the BBC in 1929 and putting his voice to new use as an announcer. On *The Kitchen Front* he found the perfect home for his warm, debonair and witty delivery. Ambrose Heath, meanwhile, was born in 1891 in north London and, to his parents' great disappointment, became a celebrated food journalist and cookery book author (his titles including *The Good Cook in Wartime*). He was also a talented cartoonist, responsible for the groundbreaking *Patsy* 'cook strip' (a comic strip with recipes presented by the eponymous young bride) and, armed with a sharp but quaint turn of phrase, fitted in well on *The Kitchen Front*.

Mabel Constanduros was a few years older than Grisewood and hailed from south London. Having made an unhappy marriage early in life, she had increasingly explored her love of writing and amateur dramatics. In 1925, she debuted an original comic creation on the BBC, *The Buggins Family*. Constanduros played all six members of the family – Grandma, Mrs, Aunt Maria, Emma, Alfie and Baby. The 'family' broadcast for twenty years from 1928, with Constanduros writing over 250 scripts. The Ministry of Food was eager to harness their popularity to pass on recipes, even though Constanduros once described Grandma as 'one of the tiresomest and crudest creatures I could imagine'. Of all the family, it was inevitably Grandma whom the public loved the most.

Other particularly popular contributors were the female double act Gert and Daisy from *Workers' Playtime*, two lovable cockney char ladies whose husbands, Bert and Wally, were in the services. They were the creations of Elsie and Doris Waters, two sisters long established on the British comedy circuit, and siblings of Horace John Waters (who, using his stage name Jack Warner, would later eclipse their fame in his lead role in *Dixon of Dock Green*).

Then there was the legendary *Radio Doctor* – 'The doctor with the greatest number of patients in the world' – whose inclusion in the programme could add millions to the audience. He was, in real life, Dr Charles Hill, the Secretary of the British Medical Association. In a tone not unreminiscent of Robert Robinson, he was able to broadcast the most disarming material in such a kindly, jovial way that he rarely offended even the most buttoned-up of listeners. He was particularly adept at dealing with issues of the gut, for instance telling his listeners: 'Visit the throne at the same time each day, whether you feel like it or not.'

The wireless also allowed for the spread of popular songs in a way previously unthinkable, and the war years produced a number of ditties that took inspiration from the food situation. Take, for instance, such numbers as Louis Jordan's 'Ration Blues', Harry Roy's 'When Can I Have a Banana Again' (both 1943) and Elsie Carlisle's 'Please Leave my Butter Alone' (1939), with its cheeky lyrics:

> Everybody says I'm old-fashioned
> To sit on the things that are rationed.
> So pinch all my ham
> And my plum and apple jam
> But please leave my butter alone.

It was natural enough, then, that Dig for Victory should have its very own anthem:

Dig! Dig! Dig! And your muscles will grow big,
Keep on pushing the spade.
Don't mind the worms,
Just ignore their squirms
And when your back aches, laugh with glee
And keep on diggin'
Till we give our foes a wiggin'.
Dig! Dig! Dig! To Victory.

While much less glamorous than the other media discussed here, the power of books, magazines and newspapers to reach vast numbers of people should not be overlooked. A 1943 social survey reported that 80 per cent of civilian adults read a newspaper daily, rising to 90 per cent on Sundays. The autumn 1942 Ministry of Agriculture review of the impact of the Dig for Victory campaign had also revealed that 77 per cent of respondents regularly read newspaper gardening notes. The report's authors commented that 'this appears to be the principle source of gardening knowledge', with the *Daily Express* (home of Mr Middleton's column) the most commonly cited title.

The Ministry of Agriculture's own Advisory Publicity Committee would in due course report: '… despite newsprint difficulties … the press has supported the campaign most gallantly'. Many gardening columnists beside Mr Middleton became household names, such as Percy Izzard at the *Daily Mail* (said by son Ralph, incidentally, to have inspired the character William Boot in Evelyn Waugh's *Scoop*) and Albert Gurie at the *News Chronicle*. Izzard memorably championed the campaign in 1940 thus: 'When once men experience the proud pleasure and the material and physical benefit of supplying their home tables with vegetables of their own cultivation they are not likely to abandon their venture into the world's oldest craft.' There were comic strips too, notably Cyril Cowell's 'Adam the Gardener' in the *Express* and Ambrose Heath's 'Digwell' in the *Daily Mirror*.

The press was also a vital outlet for officially sanctioned information, such as the Ministry of Food's 'Food Facts', available as government pamphlets but most widely read because of their inclusion in all the major newspapers and in the *Radio Times*. A typical advert for the series, aimed predominantly at the nation's housewives, ran: 'If he's fed up with his food, she gets the blame. But there are always new ideas about in Food Facts. It's in all the papers every week.'

There were other joint ventures between government and Fleet Street. The Ministry of Agriculture provided weekly gardening insertions for the Sunday national newspapers and the larger regionals for all but the eight coldest weeks of the year. In 1941, the Ministry of Food and the *Sunday Pictorial* combined in a search for the twenty 'best housewives in Britain', all of whom, of course, were doing exactly the right things on the Kitchen Front. Woolton's men devised a competition the following year to be played out in the press and judged by thirty leading chefs to find the nation's best new potato-based recipes. Meanwhile, Hannah Hudson, wife of the Minister of Agriculture, was featured in *Vogue* in a Dig for Victory pinafore.

There was also an avalanche of new books to assist growers and cooks at every level. As Tom Williams, the Ministry of Agriculture's Parliamentary Secretary, wrote in the foreword to the 1942 publication, *Gardeners Are Asking* ... 'There is a great thirst for knowledge on the purely practical points of the "Dig for Victory" Campaign, which aims at making more and more householders more dependent on the fruits of their own labours.' For the average grower, the Royal Horticultural Society's *The Vegetable Garden Displayed* was the indispensable bible. But there were plenty more to choose from, including collected volumes from the newspaper columnists, and T. W. Sanders's *Kitchen Garden and Allotment*, which returned after having first appeared in the Great War. Other tomes included George Pollitt's stirringly titled *Britain Can Feed Herself*, F. W. P. Carter's *Food Growing, Storing and Cooking* and G. H. Copley's *How to Make and Manage an Allotment*.

Other authors made it quite clear that it was every able person's duty to get stuck into the campaign as an act of defiance against the Nazis. Raymond A. Cook's *Plots Against Hitler* began: 'It is becoming increasingly obvious that, amongst the plots calculated to bring Nazism to its knees, those measuring 300 square yards are destined to play an important part.' Perhaps even more exquisitely named was *Cloches versus Hitler*, a title so ridiculous as to be magnificent. It was authored by Charles Wyse-Gardner. He could not have been called anything else …

Other authors were more interested in the produce once it had found its way into the kitchen. Constance Spry, previously better known for her flower arranging than her veg patch know-how, published *Come into the Garden, Cook* in 1942, with the following rebuke:

The fact is, vegetables in many kitchens are not taken seriously. A cook who would think it a shame to send up a flat soufflé or a lumpy sauce will with engaging cheerfulness ruin the crispest celery, the most succulent broccoli, boil green vegetables to a pulp, and tell you, when the garden is full to overflowing, that there is nothing, owing to the eccentricities of Lord Woolton, that she can think of for lunch.

Vegetable cookery of the highest order, as the French know it, for instance, has nothing to do with the complicated dishes to be found in some books under the heading of vegetarian cookery; nothing whatever to do with the lentil cutlet, vegetable turkey, or mock anything at all. It is not difficult but it does involve attention to detail. That perfection of simplicity which repays so very well is only achieved if time and trouble are taken. Technical skill is not essential.

Eleanour Sinclair Rohde was another of the great names. A renowned gardener and garden historian, her works included *Hay Box Cookery* (1939), *The Wartime Vegetable Garden* (1940) and *Culinary and Salad Herbs* (1940). She would eventually serve as the President of the Society of Women Journalists. A colleague at the *Star* was Hilda Neild who began *Wartime Cookery* (1941) with a rallying cry: 'The women's Kitchen Army is one of the most important sections of the women's fighting forces, though the members of it have no official status, wear no distinctive uniform, armlets or Service badges ...'.

Amongst the wonderful advice on offer, there were some distinctly peculiar contributions. *Food without Fuss* by Josephine Terry, for instance, included such dubious delights as carrot bread, herring and potato mustard, and pink potato soup. Elsewhere, the Vicomte de Mauduit's pamphlet, *They Can't Ration These*, presented recipes for preparing frogs, hedgehogs, sparrows and squirrels.

One of the most fun titles was *A Kitchen Goes to War*, published by John Miles Ltd in 1940 and including 150 ration-time recipes by famous people. Mr Middleton's contribution was typically understated – stuffed potatoes with butter, milk and seasoning, 'even an egg if you feel extravagant'. The stellar list of contributors included John Gielgud, Stella Gibbons, Joyce Grenfell, Jack Hobbs and Dr Marie Stopes. Sir Malcom Campbell, somewhat unimaginatively, proffered fried bacon, Mrs Neville Chamberlain fish and leek pudding, and Agatha Christie her trademark 'mystery potatoes'. Arthur Askey offered his take on haggis, a recipe he claimed came from Mrs Bagwash, the fictional char lady from his popular radio show *Band Wagon*. 'I thank you!' indeed. With such a wealth of literature available, there could not have been a Digger for Victory anywhere able to claim they were starved of information.

The other great mass medium of the age was the cinema. In 1943, a social survey revealed that 70 per cent of adults went to the cinema 'at least sometimes', with a third making the trip every week. It was a captive audience that the government could not afford to ignore. To cater for this market, the GPO Film Unit came under the jurisdiction of the Ministry of Information's Films Division in the early stages of the war and was renamed as the Crown Film Unit. The Ministry regularly commissioned work from external commercial production companies, ad agencies and newsreel companies too.

Although the Unit's most famous film-maker was Humphrey Jennings, whose output included such notable pieces as 1941's *Words for Battle* and 1942's *Listen to Britain*, it was left to others to spread the message to Dig for Victory. The most prolific film-maker on behalf of the campaign was Margaret Thomson, one of a small group of women who had been able to break into the industry. Australian born, she studied zoology before coming to London in the mid-1930s, establishing herself as an early exponent of the *cinéma vérité* style. Her output for the growers, though never extravagantly titled, offered sound advice. It included *Growing Vegetables Indoors, Storing Vegetables Outdoors, Making a Compost Heap, Clamping Potatoes, Garden Tools* and *Saving Your Own Seeds*.

However, the most memorable of the campaign's movies was, naturally enough, called *Dig for Victory* and was produced for the Ministry by Michael Hankinson at Spectator Films. Its commentary presented a bold call to arms: 'Do you like standing in a queue for your vegetables – or do you think it's tiring and a waste of valuable time? Do you ever find your long wait has been useless – that supplies of what you want have run out before your turn comes? It's not the greengrocer's fault. It's up to you. Dig for Victory!'

There were a good many other titles directed at the garden army, among them: *All About Carrots, Backyard Front, Bampton Shows the Way* (a film about a Devonshire village preparing for a 'Food Week'), *Filling the Gap, Garden Friends and Foes, Growing Good Potatoes, How to Dig* (the first of six films produced in conjunction with the Royal Horticultural Society, with commentary by Roy Hay), *Roots of Victory* and *Simple Fruit Pruning*.

In 1942, the Ministry of Agriculture persuaded the Greenford and Northolt Allotment Gardens Committee to contribute a film of their own. The Committee's chairman, Councillor A. J. Johnson, made an address direct to camera. He cut a rather plump and jovial figure, with the slightest hint of pomposity. 'Ladies and gentlemen, to make a successful appearance on a film there is some mystic quality known as SA,' he began. 'SA' was the popularly used abbreviation for sex appeal, a characteristic not obviously bursting forth from Mr Johnson. 'Well, this address is an SA in as much as it is a Spade Appeal, an appeal for more spadework in this district.' He went on to celebrate 'the health-giving properties there are in vegetables taken from the plot to the pot.'

Another film was made in support of the first Dig for Victory pamphlet and its call for all-year planting. Featuring a man being served by a waiter wielding a deathly scythe, it included the following admonitory couplets:

> In Spring this gardener sowed away,
> He meant to eat well every day …
> Came the Winter, table bare,
> He couldn't eat what wasn't there …
> The dreadful fate of this poor man
> Was due to lack of garden plan.

However, the films that had most impact on those concerned with food were the *Food Flashes*, of which some two hundred were made for the Ministry of Food between March 1942 and November 1946, each one with an average estimated audience of twenty million. Each was only fifteen seconds long, offering a useful tip on making the best of the available food in a punchy and humorous way, often using famous faces like 'Cheerful' Charlie Chester. A great many were made by Cecil Hepworth, one of the pioneers of pre-First World War cinematography who had effectively gone into retirement in the 1920s but returned to the business to contribute his talent to the propaganda drive. In 1950, he was one of the first six Fellows of the British Film Academy. One of the films, devoted to the cooking of greens, hints at the light tone of the series: 'Thanks to the weather and – yes, old man – the growers, we have wonderful supplies of fresh vegetables just now. But don't murder the vitamins now, will you. Boil quickly in very little water …'. They played an important role in fostering the climate in which people learned to love their home-grown produce.

For a nation that had to some extent fallen out of love with the soil over the preceding two centuries, reigniting that passion for the fat of their own land was the challenge that faced those in charge of the campaign. As *Wise Eating in Wartime*, a collection of advice from *Kitchen Front* broadcasts, had it: 'Today we are interested in food as never before. It's taken a war to make us interested, but that's by the way.'

Government officials and members of the creative industries harnessed the potential of all the media available to them and won over popular opinion through a mixture of practical advice, good humour, poignancy and appeals to the public's sense of duty. It was a job done with consummate brilliance by professionals prepared to mine their own pools of creativity to produce work that, technical advances apart, stands up impressively to the scrutiny of our own multi-media age.

13. Nothing So Good as Digging

With the public behind the campaign, the media operation at full pelt and administration at both the national and local levels running as smoothly as it could realistically be hoped, the golden age of Dig for Victory extended from 1941 through to early 1944, with participation levels peaking in 1942–3. Under Winston Churchill's guidance, and after a bumpy first few months in office when Britain seemed to be the last man standing against the German onslaught, any sense that the nation was doomed to defeat died away. For the first time since the declaration of war, victory seemed at least possible and the willingness among ordinary people to do all they could towards that end only increased.

The authorities strived hard to maintain a sense of urgency but not panic. On 19 April 1943, the *Citizen*, a Gloucestershire local paper, reported on a speech given by Viscount Bledisloe, the President of the Gloucestershire Home Food Production Society. He warned that the country was 'faced, during the coming twelve months, with the most critical period in the matter of food that this nation has ever experienced,' and that '… no countryman who had a plot of land, however small, had any right or title to purchase vegetables in town shops'.

He then took a moment to praise the achievements of the government thus far, before reiterating the importance of small-scale production:

> If we fail to realise it and are inclined to be complacent it is no doubt due to the wise and sensible administration of the Ministries of Food and Agriculture. Every foreigner who comes into this country ... exclaims with surprise and delight at the way in which we as a nation are being fed during this war. There is nothing to touch it in any other part of the world ... While it is clear that the business of feeding the community must rest with the farmers and commercial growers, it is the conviction of those who founded it [The Home Food Production Society] that the 'little man' who cultivates a garden, keeps a pig, or breeds rabbits can, by his very number, contribute substantially to the national larder.

A survey conducted by *The Economist* magazine in 1944 probed the reasons why people had decided to pick up their spades. Over 50 per cent said the principle reason was to produce fresh food for themselves, their family and friends, a further 20 per cent pointed towards their love of 'fresh air' or because it was a way to save money. Only a fifth of people cited 'working to help war effort'. But that was, after all, a vital aspect of the campaign and one which should not be under-estimated or besmirched.

In 1941's gardening guide, *Plots Against Hitler*, Raymond A. Cook seemed to suggest that the greatest reward was a spiritual one:

> God bless us through work – through the knowledge and expertise gained thereby – through an increase in our material resources –

through the pride that comes with the knowledge that we are an asset and not a liability to our fellow-men – through a sense of pride in work well done – and finally, because we are sharing with Him the joy of creation, 'in helping the earth to bring forth her increase'.

Rob Hudson summed it up neatly at the relaunch of the Dig for Victory Campaign in September 1940: 'I can assure you, there's nothing so good as digging.'

Health was regularly cited by the authorities as a further reason to get involved. Indeed, one of the early official slogans for the campaign was 'Fighting Fit!' It was a subject particularly beloved of the Department of Food. The following is a typical statement released by Lord Woolton's Department in 1942 extolling the value of the humble spud:

The importance of home-grown food is already greater than at any time in the last war ... Potatoes are one of the most useful of the home-grown foods, and one giving energy and bodily warmth as well as protection against illness ... Scientists have stressed that we would do well to eat 12 ozs of potatoes per head each day instead of 8 ozs as at present.

It is striking that the talk was almost exclusively about vegetables, rather than fruit. For a nation famed for its orchards and its love of fruit pies and crumbles, this might at first seem odd, but the logic was sound. Hudson was asked in the Commons in February 1941 'whether he will include the growing of fruit in the "Grow more food" campaign, now his Department has recognised its value in our national diet?' His response: 'As fruit trees or bushes cannot furnish any appreciable contribution to the food supply within a reasonable time, I do not feel justified in encouraging new plantings.' And so it was. Newly planted hard fruits – apples, cherries, pears and plums – required a good three or four years before they would offer up a half-decent crop, and even bush fruits such as blackcurrants and raspberries need a couple of years to bed in. So for the most part, vegetables it was (although some growers also turned their hands to harvesting their own tobacco, particularly after it was subject to a hefty tax increase in 1942).

There were many other memorable slogans, like 'An ounce of salad is worth an inch of lipstick' – presumably one aimed largely at the nation's housewives! However, as Joan Strange reveals in her diary entry for 28 September 1943, not everyone was convinced by such arguments. 'One of my lady patients stuck me out by saying we're half-starved!' she noted. 'I said I'd not lost an ounce during the war and that my teeth had not decayed so much during these four years! The wartime diet is excellent from a health point of view.'

Nor was an opportunity missed to promote the direct health benefits of gardening itself. Tucked away in a 1943 Ministry of Health publication called *How to Keep Well in Wartime* was a section offering advice on keeping mind and body active. Under the heading 'Muscles are Meant to be Used,' it suggested ways to keep muscles from 'becoming set', advocating that readers use their weekends to 'walk, cycle, swim, *dig*, row a boat and enjoy it' [author's italics].

There were, of course, practical problems to overcome. Growing is hard enough in peacetime; in wartime it requires still greater determination and innovation. Churchill had, however, helped foster a spirit of 'backs to the wall', a position, as others have noted, that often brings out the best in the British people. Arguably, no social group proved themselves a more resilient bunch during the war than those who took up the spade in the interests of Digging for Victory.

Growers embraced the challenges they faced, gaining satisfaction from finding solutions to problems and becoming ever more adventurous in their growing. ('If you have never tried garlic, plant a row and see what you think of it,' wrote Mr Middleton in April 1940. 'You don't need much; a little goes a long way.') The results were, broadly, far better than the campaign's overlords could ever have hoped. As Middleton noted in the *Daily Express* as early as 13 July 1940: 'When I prowl about allotments one of my objects is to look for faults and suggest improvements ... But I must congratulate the army of new diggers on their efforts, for in spite of my criticisms the vast majority of plots are looking much better than anything I had anticipated.'

As the war progressed, there were predictable shortages of seeds. By 1941, Suttons Seeds, one of the giants of the industry, was running adverts explaining: 'The "Dig for Victory" Campaign has increased enormously the demand for "SUTTONS SEEDS", and although we have very large stocks of seed we strongly advise early ordering, to make sure of obtaining your favourite varieties.' By the end of the year, *The Times* was reporting, 'A serious shortage of suitable seed ...' This was not an utter disaster – one can, after all, persuade a potato or a tomato to provide you with everything you need to sow a new crop. It was, though, indicative of the circumstances that faced growers.

The introduction to the 1943 catalogue for Ryder's Seeds of St Albans adds to the picture of hardship:

Absolute austerity has been the keystone in the compilation and production of this 1943 issue of Ryder's General Catalogue ...

It is absolutely clear that paper is needed for the war effort, and the sooner that effort is successful, the sooner can we return to elaborate catalogues to serve the gardens of our country at peace … When hostilities are over we hope to help you once more in brightening your borders.

Literally no pastime – even studying the seed catalogue – remained the idle pleasure it might once have been.

Among other more pressing problems was a shortage of suitable fertilisers. In this regard, many of the solutions favoured by the Diggers for Victory might struggle to comply with the most stringent modern standards of health and safety or of ecological concern. To begin with, the situation had been manageable and there were reasonable supplies of, for instance, dried blood, hoof and horn meal, and meat and bone meal. Those close to suitable coastal regions took to using seaweed. There were also fairly plentiful supplies of animal manure though, as one would expect, the growers in rural areas were rather bettered catered for in this regard than those in the towns. It was not an uncommon sight in larger cities to see neighbours racing each other down the streets with shovels, hoping to be the first to get to the excreta deposited by the delivery horse of the milkman or coal man. However, as animal-feed stocks deteriorated, feed was manufactured using the contents of scrap bins, into which the public would dispose of all sorts of material, both organic and inorganic, despite clear instructions to separate waste out. This led to the emergence of a curious substance known as London dung, which was infamous for its peculiar smell and for visible evidence of materials including paper and, on occasion, bits of old corset!

As the war continued, supplies of traditional fertilisers grew ever scarcer. Potash, which before the war had been imported in vast quantities from Germany and several other north European countries, became a great rarity. The government issued instructions that it was to be used only on those crops that particularly benefitted from it, such as tomatoes. The Ministry of Agriculture also advised growers on how to produce their own supplies by collecting the wood ash from a bonfire (which could burn beneath a layer of soil to eradicate the risk of visible smouldering during blackouts). Gardeners were also encouraged to treat their soil with lime to ensure its 'sweetness'.

Many households became highly adept at making their own compost by recycling fruit and vegetable peelings and other household organic waste. On 2 March 1940, the *Daily Express* published a letter from a Mr L. Bizley of Surbiton detailing an idea for a present for one's spouse. Though it rated low on the romance stakes, the letters editor considered the advice strong enough to award Mr Bizley a guinea for it. 'Cabbage stumps, orange peel, and so on thrown on the compost heap decay dead slowly,' our correspondent wrote, 'so buy your wife a new mincing machine ... All peelings and coarse waste can be quickly put through the machine to produce a pulp that will almost immediately be available as manure.'

But it became apparent to the authorities that there was a compelling argument for using artificial fertilisers. From 1942 the government-standard National Growmore fertiliser became available, a balanced formula that included 7 per cent each of potash, nitrogen and phosphate. Allotment holders were able to claim 42 lbs of the stuff, either through registered merchants or via their local allotment society. That quantity had been calculated in order to provide 30 lbs to dress a typical 10-rod plot, with 12 lbs over to provide potatoes, winter greens and spring cabbages with an extra dressing.

The keen grower then faced a daunting array of pests and other potential threats to crops that were, on balance, regarded as marginally less heinous than the Nazis themselves, although at times it was close run. The government and the popular press regularly made the association between nature's more aggressive pests and Hitler's armies. In 1940, the *Daily Express* responded to reports that rabbits had caused expensive damage to grass and grain by running a story under the title, 'Herr Rabbit – Fifth Columnist'. Elsewhere, millipedes were depicted in cartoons adorned with swastikas while rats were pictured sporting tiny Hitler toothbrush-moustaches beneath their twitching rodent noses. The common or garden house sparrow came in for some of the most brutal treatment, particularly in 1942 when the Ministry of Agriculture insti-gated a campaign to get rid of 'Hitler's feathered friend'. The Ministry denounced the breed unrestrainedly as 'the allot-ment holders' chief enemy'. 'This year sparrows have been specially active,' ran the warnings. 'Householders are asked to destroy them ruthlessly.'

A great many of the pesticides and fungicides available at the time and actively promoted by experts were not for the faint-hearted, and are unlikely to be found in the potting sheds of the modern, environmentally sensitive cultivator. Take, for instance, Derris powder, a source of rotenone commonly used to protect peas, which was subsequently found to have such high levels of toxicity that it is no longer legally available. Other products required gardeners to sign the poison book at the chemist when they purchased them. These included cyanide (it is worth remembering that the Zyklon B used in Hitler's death camps was cyanide-based), nicotine in solution and sulphuric acid (to be sprayed on onions!).

Two of the most popular fungicides, and particularly favoured by the Ministry of Agriculture, were the Burgundy and Bordeaux mixtures. Both were named after the respective French wine-growing regions where they had been developed for use in vineyards in the nineteenth century. Burgundy mixture is a solution of copper sulphate and sodium carbonate, particularly useful on trees and bushes. Bordeaux mixture, on the other hand, is a mixture of copper sulphate and hydrated lime, and is highly effective against potato blight. Both solutions can, however, lead to potentially dangerous, high volumes of copper in the ground around treated plants and have subsequently been implicated in the pollution of waterways and the harming of fish and livestock.

Other new skills had to be learned quickly, such as the making of one's own hessian sacks when commercial supplies dwindled. Shirley Brown, who lived in West London during the war, recalled how an activity as basic even as watering required a more circumspect approach:

I am just amazed at how much water is used these days on gardens because where these allotments were there was only one water tap. So if you wanted to water something, you had to fill a can and carry it to where it was needed. The old gardeners would keep the hoe going to loosen the soil and everything grew well. The roots would then go down and find moisture.

In conditions of adversity, firm bonds of friendship formed among growers. It is perhaps above all else the sense of social cohesion created by the campaign that has ensured Dig for Victory lives on in the national memory.

Joan Strange, for one, was taken under the collective wing of two elderly gents who worked the plot next to hers. One of them even penned some verse that he presented to her:

> Lord Woolton to my mind is quite a hero,
> Contrasted with that other German Nero;
> So take to digging, not as a source of wealth,
> But England, home and beauty and for health.
> Though meatless meals may lack your special gravy,
> Just think of how you spare our matchless Navy.

Inevitably, even the keenest of gardeners tired of the hard graft now and again. For instance, few ever claimed particularly fond memories of harvesting frost-covered Brussels sprouts, a job best done with ungloved hands, virtually guaranteeing the grower painful, cold-bitten fingers as they twisted the vegetables free from their tough trunks. But for most growers, hard work was a price they were prepared to pay not only for the benefit of extra food on their dinner plates, but for the joy incumbent in the job itself. In addition, there was rare pleasure to be gained in planting a spade in the soil, leaning on the handle and taking a moment to chat to friends, new and old, over the hot topics of the day or, just as commonly, to share crop-related knowledge and wisdom. For all the official advice of the government and the plentiful information available on the wireless and in the newspapers, a Ministry of Agriculture survey in early autumn 1942 revealed that fully 84.3 per cent of growers obtained advice from their fellow gardeners.

Paul Fagg was a schoolboy during the war, his family having

moved from Deal on the Kent coast to the less precariously situated village of Wye, between Ashford and Canterbury. His father had long been a keen gardener (he was growing exotic crops including asparagus on a semi-commercial basis as early as 1933), and by the time the Dig for Victory campaign started, the family was already 'doing its bit' by growing produce in their small back garden and on an allotment too. Paul remembers his mother securing supplies of seeds through the Women's Institute, which had in turn been sent stocks by the Canadian branch of the WI in a gesture of support. Among the supplies were seeds for courgettes and mangetout, neither of which Paul had eaten in any quantity before. But as well as enjoying new eating experiences, he recalled particularly fondly the simple pleasure of digging up something he had tended from seed. 'I can remember the excitement of digging small carrots on the allotment,' he reminisced, 'selecting one, cleaning it on my sleeve and biting into its fresh crispness!' He was in no doubt that Dig for Victory had played an important role in boosting morale during those dark times, concluding '... organisations such as allotment societies really do help to keep communities together'.

Meanwhile, in west London the youthful Shirley Brown was living close to Osterley Park, the family seat of the Earls of Jersey. The house had a colourful wartime history, and in 1940, the incumbent Ninth Earl gave permission to Captain Tom Wintringham to use the grounds to train aspiring members of the Home Guard in guerrilla and street-fighting tactics. Wintringham had picked up his knowledge during the Spanish Civil War, having gone out to cover the conflict as a journalist before ending up in command of the British Battalion of the Republican International Brigade. He was invalided back home in 1937.

Churchill was not keen that such a key aspect of the war effort was in the hands of a left-wing firebrand who had played an instrumental role in the 1926 General Strike and who had served a prison term for sedition and inciting soldiers to mutiny. The War Office took over the Osterley Park school's running in September 1940 and closed it down within a few months, relocating training to other locations around the country. Nonetheless, the Earl of Jersey was keen that the house should contribute to the national effort and so saw to it that the grounds were made available as allotments.

Shirley's father successfully applied to tend two plots, where he grew enough vegetables not only to feed the immediate family but to be able to make gifts to other relatives and neighbours as well. Shirley remembers that the allotments, run by the Spring Grove Allotment Association, fostered a keen sense of community. The governing committee built a makeshift hut which opened on Sunday mornings with a staff of willing volunteers providing growers with supplies of seeds and fertilisers. Despite her youth, Shirley was drafted in to help, charged with weighing out seed and then writing on the fronts of envelopes to explain which varieties were contained therein and how much they cost (typically between 1½*d.* and 3*d.*). Then there was the excitement of an annual show, as Shirley recalled:

Once a year a horticulture show was held where the Mayor and Mayoress and local dignitaries attended. The Parks and Gardens Department made a plant display along the front of the stage. One has to remember there weren't a lot of social activities in those War years and so everybody turned out for the event – with all money raised going to the British Red Cross.

While Dig for Victory was principally concerned with the cultivation of crops, it helped created an atmosphere in which the public were willing to take control of other aspects of their food supply too. People who might never have previously kept animals now started keeping beehives to produce their own honey, or reared chickens, rabbits and even pigs. Often the keeping of livestock was best undertaken by small co-operatives, bringing with it a new dimension of community participation.

At first, the government took an ambiguous line on the subject of amateur animal husbandry. There was a legitimate fear that some rations might be diverted away from the human bellies for which they were intended and given instead to little Cottontail living in a hutch in the back garden. But the Ministries of Agriculture and Food soon realised that domestic keepers might make a significant contribution towards the nation's dinner table. On 21 June 1940, *The Times* attempted to unpick the legal situation: 'Any householder or allotment holder may now keep hens, pigs, or rabbits so long as he does not create a nuisance or cause prejudice to health …'. That latter clause meant, for instance, that you could not keep cockerels ('The cock that crows at dawn would be an objectionable disturber of the peace'). However, things did not always work out as expected. The Rev. Peter Thomas recalls how his father visited a livestock market in Bath and brought home a fine-looking specimen. When Peter's mother pondered whether the creature would be a good layer, her husband assured her it would – just at the moment when it flew up on to the fridge and gave out a marvellous crow.

An Order in Council had suspended all restrictive covenants in tenancy agreements and local by-laws prohibiting the keeping of livestock. 'Thus the way is cleared,' *The Times* reported, 'for the householder to turn husbandman.' It was an entirely sensible move – such animals provided a means of recycling organic household waste, and as well as producing meat, offered the prospect of other useful by-products including eggs and, for the Digger for Victory, fresh manure.

A craze for beekeeping swept the nation as sugar rationing took its toll. Hives were no longer a rare sight in urban back gardens and appeared in great numbers on allotments where they were previously seldom found. Honey not only appeased the appetites of those cursed with a sweet tooth, but was also commonly used in the treatment of non-serious burns and wounds because of its antiseptic properties. From 1943, bee-keepers could apply to the Ministry of Food for extra sugar supplies for use in their hives (up to 10 lbs per colony over winter, and 5 lbs in the spring). But it was a system ripe for abuse and there was soon concern at the Ministry that the sugar was not making it as far as the hives. The decision was thus taken to dye it green in the hope that it would put off buyers on the black market, although the measure was quickly dropped when a proportion of beekeepers indicated that their colonies were producing lurid green honey.

A similar system of supplementary rations was available for rabbit keepers, with organised clubs able to obtain extra supplies of bran. In return the clubs agreed to sell a minimum of 50 per cent of their produce to government-approved buyers. By 1943, there were some three thousand registered clubs. Wild rabbits fared much less well than their domestic counterparts, as they were regarded as among the most destructive pests of the countryside. Official literature suggested that nine rabbits could consume as much pasture as two sheep, and farmers were encouraged to do everything in their power to get rid of as many as possible.

The introduction of the Morrison shelter in March 1941 was something of a boon for gardeners and allotment holders whose crops had been subject to rabbit attack. The shelter, named in honour of Herbert Morrison, the Home Secretary, consisted of steel mesh over a heavy frame and was designed for indoor use; if suitably draped, it could pass for a table and had room enough for up to three people. The enterprising grower, however, was quick to recognise that the mesh could also be employed outside to keep rabbits off their veg.

While wild rabbits were subject to little sentimentality, the most common problem for the domestic rabbit keeper was the propensity to grow emotionally attached to their charges. It was not an uncommon occurrence for a young girl to be told that her pet rabbit had escaped from its captivity, and then to be served up a hearty 'chicken' stew to help her get over the shock. Many reputedly did not make the link between pet and supper until years afterwards.

Meanwhile, keeping chickens could revolutionise a family's weekly menu at a time when the ration provided just one or two eggs per person per week and farm chicken numbers had fallen by 30 per cent, with farmers unwilling to fork out for costly feed. But while chicken-keeping on a commercial scale was becoming prohibitively expensive, the return against outlay for domestic keepers was considerably better. The introduction to Alan Thompson and Claude H. Goodchild's *Keeping Poultry and Rabbits on Scraps* extolled the virtues of the unlauded egg: 'The hen's egg is the finest concentrated food known to man. It is produced by a humble, and a slightly ridiculous, creature whose remarkable qualities have never been justly appreciated.'

Hen keepers could exchange their ration of shell eggs for protein-rich poultry meal, which was added to household vegetable scraps before being fed to hens. Karswood Poultry Spice, which contained ground insects, was another popular supplement given to assist with laying. A household keeping fewer than twenty hens was permitted to keep whatever eggs were produced without having to contribute a share to official stocks. Though in reality few families had the resources to keep more than about five birds, this was an efficient way of bypassing at least one wartime shortage and avoided an excessive reliance on the dreaded dried egg. At a Dig for Victory show held in Huddersfield in 1942, it was reported that three people had breakfasted on one hen's egg, a fine specimen with three yolks and a shell deemed worthy of public display.

And if Mother did not want to use all her fresh eggs at once, she could undertake to preserve them in isinglass solution. A gelatinous substance made from the swim bladders of fish, isinglass could keep eggs fresh for up to a year, though with the downside that some claimed the eggs developed a slightly fishy taste and, should the solution find its way onto anything other than the eggs themselves, it was the Devil's own job to get rid of the stain. By 1943, a quarter of the fresh eggs consumed in the United Kingdom came from home coops, and at its peak the Domestic Poultry Keeper's Council had over 1.75 million members keeping 12 million birds.

The swill used to feed these domestic stocks represented a perfect way to recycle household scraps. Favoured ingredients included the peelings from potatoes and other vegetables, pods from peas and beans, bacon rind and cabbage leaves. Everyone was encouraged to contribute such waste, with local authorities making regular collections from households not using their

scraps to feed their own animals. A note on the correct preparation of swill even found its way into the lyrics of a popular
song of the time:

> I'm feeding the calves
> And the pigs and the hens
> (Yes, I carefully boil all the swill)
> And the cows and the horses,
> The sheep and the ducks
> Oh, the coupons are tiresome, but still
> The hens go on laying,
> The pigs are eight score.
> My word, we are
> Winning the war!

Once a chicken's laying days were over, it too could be
recycled in the form of a tasty Sunday roast. To share such a
delight with friends or neighbours was a significant gesture. Ann
Sadler, then a young schoolgirl living in Ebley, Gloucestershire,
retained a poem sent by her family, the Millards, to their
neighbours, the Teagles, concerning the gift of a hen called
Belinda. Despite Belinda's unenviable end, she may at least have
been comforted by the knowledge that she helped bring the two
families together, their relationship evidently underpinned by
kindness, amiability and genuine warmth. The poem, entitled
'The Lay of the Last-But-One Minstrel', ran thus:

> To Teagles all
> Both large and small
> I bring the Millards' Greeting!
> And tho' I'm old,

I make so bold,
To trust I'll be good eating.

Into the pot
With water hot,
My carcass gently seating,
You'd better boil,
But do not spoil
By over much of heating.

Then into the oven
I'd best be shoven,
With sausage and force-meating
To nicely roast
As brown as toast,
Two hours or so completing.

Serve on hot plate
And don't be late,
For time will soon be fleeting.
If all is done
As I have sung
I e'en will take some beating.

In short order came the 'Response' from the Teagles.

For Mam and Daddy Millard
And Ann and David too
The Teagles send their greetings
And Gran, 'The same to you'.

When knock came on the 'winder'
And then upon the door,
We didn't 'spect Belinda,
Our old good friend of yore.

And now that we have seen her
Unfrocked and laid in state,
It makes our poor eyes water
To mourn Belinda – late.

Away with tears and mourning,
Belinda's work is done,
And now she adds the crowning
To Christmas fare and fun.

We'll take good care in cooking
To follow what you say,
By constant watch and looking
At Beeton and your lay.

And then as thanks we render
For such a lovely bird
We'll say 'My, ain't she tender
A chicken! 'Pon my word!

Perhaps the most famous examples of small-scale domestic livestock-keeping were the pig clubs. It could on occasions be a chaotic business (as immortalised by Alan Bennett in the 1984 BAFTA-winning movie, *A Private Function*) but it was crucial in lessening the impact of vastly reduced levels of commercial meat production. One of the greatest properties of a pig is that virtually the whole animal can be consumed ('bar its eyes and its squeak' as the popular saying went). Aside from many tasty cuts of meat, its head could be cooked up into a nourishing brawn, its trotters and chitterlings (innards) boiled, and its fat turned into lard, a tasty substitute when butter was short. In December 1940, *The Times* extolled the pure pleasure of porcine husbandry: '... for those who have little time to spare and sometimes feel harassed by the rush of these days, a pen of pigs, especially after they have enjoyed a meal of kitchen waste, presents a restful picture and an antidote to worry.' The pig was, after all, 'a cleanly and comely animal' when kept in decent conditions.

By that stage there were already almost 250 registered clubs, comprising 6,500 members and some 5,000 pigs. From the earliest days of the war it had been apparent that commercial keepers were finding the upkeep of their animals a major financial strain, whereas individuals or small groups were in a far stronger position to take the creatures on. The movement to that point had been particularly strong in Hertfordshire, Lincolnshire and Surrey. The interests of clubs were represented by the Small Pig Keepers' Council, which negotiated with the government over terms of membership, worked with local councils to ensure that animals were properly kept, and assisted members with advice, cut-price feed and the collection of scraps for swill.

There were two distinct types of club. In the first, individual members looked after their own animals and could kill up to two pigs a year for their personal use, although the animals had to be dispatched by a government-registered slaughterer. A domestic pig-keeper could also sell to a local retail butcher any remaining meat (up to a whole side) at a price not exceeding the wholesale price. The second type of club involved members looking after one or more animals in a cooperative – often attached to a company, mine, school or other social group, and commonly utilising canteen waste in the animal feed. Members could claim half of the meat produced for themselves but were expected to sell the other half to government-approved retailers. In reality, 62 per cent of the meat produced by individual pig-keepers found its way to market while cooperatives sold on 75 per cent.

In the early days of the war, a lack of knowledge concerning the preservation of meat was an issue. The Small Pig-Keepers Council therefore published *Home-Curing of the Pig and Use of By-products* in 1940. It eventually talked the Ministry of Food into allowing Pig Club pigs to be sent to bacon factories for professional curing, the Ministry having initially been reluctant because of the logistical implications.

The sight of pig bins for the depositing of scraps was a common one on street corners throughout the war and for a good many years afterwards. In 1943, Whyteways Cyder Co. Ltd paid for adverts in the press, encouraging contributions with the following verse (based on an old Devonshire rhyme):

> Dearly beloved brethren, it is not a sin,
> When ye peel potatoes, to throw away the skin,
> The skins feed the pigs, and the pigs feed we,
> Dearly beloved brethren, what think ye?

According to official estimates, the scraps from about fifteen households, when mixed with a little meal, were sufficient to feed one pig. Many councils were excellent at collecting and emptying the bins regularly (smaller towns, including Watford, earned especial praise) but collections were less reliable in some big cities. On hot days, the stench from an unemptied bin could be overwhelming, and there were reports of receptacles oozing a strange yellow gunge.

The bins were also the subject of regular horror stories that they harboured coins, bottle tops, glass shards and even razor blades, with disastrous consequences for any pig unlucky enough to come across such items in their feeding troughs, but on the whole the system worked well. Occasionally the pigs' diets might be bolstered in some areas by the addition of acorns. One schoolmaster in Westmorland regularly sent out his pupils to gather acorns, and in return for their hard work, the children received six-penny shares in the school Pig Club.

In the early part of the war, many eager club members were stymied by the lack of suitable land and materials for constructing sties but still the scheme built up an impressive head of steam. In May 1941, the King and Queen reportedly encouraged members of the royal household to establish a club which was, conveniently, the thousandth to be registered. It was said to have passed on two-thirds of its meat to the Ministry of Food. By August 1943, there were over 5,000 clubs throughout the United Kingdom with 110,000 members looking after 120,000 pigs. At the war's finish, the clubs were producing over 10,000 tons of meat every year. It was a remarkable return, especially when set against the largely unsuccessful attempts to institute a similar programme in the Great War (though there were a few exceptions such as a club at Maisemore in Gloucestershire that ran without a break from one war to the next).

The best known of all the pig clubs was a pioneering branch set up in the first months of the war by dustmen from Tottenham, who were keen to find a use for at least some of the waste they were dealing with on a daily basis. The experimental scheme was scrutinised by officials from the Ministries of Health, Agriculture and Food. Within its first three weeks of operation the dustmen had obtained enough food not only for their own pigs but to supply other pig dealers with 10 tons of feed. The club was presented as an example to others, and the contents of pig bins came to be known as Tottenham pudding. Other clubs that gained their fair share of attention included that of the Chelsea police and the piggery in Hyde Park.

A Ministry of Food advertisement encouraging the public to save their scraps pays fitting tribute to the contribution made by the pig clubs:

Because of the pail,
The scraps were saved;
Because of the scraps,
The pigs were saved;
Because of the pigs,
The rations were saved;
Because of the rations,
The ships were saved;
Because of the ships,
The island was saved;
Because of the island,
The Empire was saved;
And all because of
The housewife's pail.

14. Pulling Together

By 1941, Dig for Victory had become a mass movement and a brilliant example of social cohesion. While the individual working away in the back garden undoubtedly had a role to play and could carry on his enterprise in relative seclusion, there was a growing realisation that still more could be achieved by gardeners combining their efforts in cooperative enterprises. Two notable case studies pay ample testament to the advantages of working together.

Ann Sadler, mentioned in the previous chapter, was the daughter of Walter Millard, the Honorary Secretary of the Home Food Production Club in Ebley, Gloucestershire. He was instrumental in establishing a potato cooperative in Gloucestershire, something of a landmark project that offered a blueprint for similar schemes, particularly in rural areas.

After some discussion, club members decided that it was wasteful and uneconomic for each of them to plant potatoes crops in their own gardens. Additionally, it was pointed out that if they combined their efforts to plant at least a full acre's worth between them, they would qualify for a £10 government subsidy entitlement (worth almost £300 today). The motion was passed to establish a cooperative planting scheme, with a sub-committee set up to find a suitable area of wasteland. Despite Gloucestershire's not inconsiderable area, this task proved among the most difficult aspects of the whole enterprise but eventually a plot of unused ground was identified. Millard discussed the project in a broadcast of the BBC's *Back to the Land* in October 1942. He explained: '... a piece of land which might seem an impossible one for a farmer to work with his limited labour and many acres of land, is quite a different proposition for a group of householders working in cooperation. Here the labour is almost unlimited and although individually we are busy people – I'm a schoolmaster, for example – we found the whole scheme, apart from harvesting the crop, only demanded a total of eight to ten hours from each of us during the whole season.'

Indeed, the planting of a ton of potatoes took only just over two hours when shared among the group. Membership of the project was initially open to forty members, each of whom was required to put down 5s. at the outset for their 'share' of the project. In the event, the scheme quickly became over-subscribed to the point that several people had to be turned away. There was much hard work to be done but still there was time for good humour. Millard recalled:

> The earthing up was not without its humorous side. One man, finding himself with the morning off, went down to the plot to earth up his row. He took off his jacket and set to work. When the job was finished he put on his jacket and lit a pipe and stood up to admire his work. Then he discovered he had hoed up the next man's rows! However, it so happened that the other was working very long hours, so a packet of cigarettes soon put this right.

By the culmination of the project, each member had paid 14*s*., although 3*s*. 6*d*. of this was covered by subsidy, so final outlay amounted to a not excessive 10*s*. 6*d*. per shareholder. In return, they could lay claim to 'six or seven hundredweights of first-class potatoes', as well as taking pride in the satisfaction of a job remarkably well done.

But there is perhaps no single story that better encapsulates the power of the Dig for Victory campaign to galvanise a community than that of the Bethnal Green Bombed Sites Association. When in 1941 Cook dedicated *Plots Against Hitler*, to 'the people of the South-East who for more than a year have lived and worked under shell-fire', the population of Bethnal Green were among the most deserving of his recognition. Nestled in the heart of east London, few neighbourhoods suffered more during the course of the war, particularly from the terrors of German aerial bombing. It is estimated that some 80 tons of bombs fell on the area over the course of the war, leaving at least 550 of its residents dead and a further 400 seriously injured. Around 22,000 homes were damaged, over 2,200 of which were completely destroyed and a further 1,000 rendered unlivable.

And yet, for all the extreme suffering it had to endure in those years, Bethnal Green did not buckle but instead came to epitomise the 'Blitz spirit'. Drawing on a collective will that refused to be daunted, the community instead sought ways to cope with its hardships and make life as bearable as possible. So on the afternoon of Friday 24 April 1942, there was a meeting held at Bethnal Green Town Hall of 'persons interested in the development of Bombed Sites in Bethnal Green'. Chaired by Councillor Brig. Gen. Sir Wyndham Deedes, it was 'for the purpose of considering as to what steps could be taken for the development of bombed sites in the Borough, which had been cleared or mainly cleared of buildings, for the purpose of providing amenities, and also for the production of food'. This was something the residents of the area had already got to grips with on a rather more ad hoc basis some while earlier, with a BBC broadcast talk by the Ministry of Agriculture in September 1941 describing how 'Bethnal Green people have dug up the concrete playground of a bombed school to get land to grow vegetables ...'

The April 1942 gathering drew sufficient interest for a Bombed Sites Association to be established, which met for its inaugural meeting on 1 June 1942. Sir Wyndham was appointed as chairman of the governing committee. In his opening address he talked of the large numbers of local people keen to grow their own vegetables but who had little chance of obtaining a suitable site, since nearby Victoria Park had already been turned over to allotment plots and was virtually at capacity.

At the initial April meeting, nine sites had been identified as fit for development (including Nos. 279 to 289, Globe Road, which one Miss Monckton had earmarked for the rearing of pigs). By the June meeting, the number had risen to eighteen, and by the end of the month the Association was in active negotiations over thirty-two sites. In addition, the committee had secured a promise from the Metropolitan Gardens Association that they would send one of their horticultural advisers to provide them with the benefit of his experience. There was also the donation of some basic tools from Oxford House, a local charitable organisation set up in 1884 at the behest of Keble College, Oxford to give its staff and graduates some understanding of the difficulties faced by the urban poor. The Women's Voluntary Service made an additional early gift of gardening equipment.

The Association's core aims were threefold: to promote the interests of its member allotment holders and gardeners; to provide support and instruction; and to conduct negotiations in respect of land issues. Its motto was simple: 'Quality and not Quantity.' The cost of membership was set at an affordable rate that encouraged inclusivity. In the first year it stood at 1s. per annum, remaining at that level until 1943 when it was raised to 2s. Clearly it did the trick, as the Association's membership had swelled to two hundred by early October 1942, and was double that again by the time of the 1943 annual report. By then the Association was overseeing three hundred individual allotments, which covered some 10½ acres of land. It also boasted an impressive array of specially constructed housing for livestock, which included 4,000 rabbits, 2,000 chickens, 10 pigs, 9 goats, and a handful of ducks and geese. By 1944, the Association had attracted such fame that when it undertook a programme of livestock slaughter in time for the Christmas season, the event garnered coverage in the national press.

As well as media interest, the Association also attracted goodwill from all sorts of quarters, which often translated into financial and other donations. In its early months the Association was able to persuade the local council to make a gift of the manure heap that resided in Bethnal Green's Ion Square Gardens. Another anonymous donor gave £120 (just short of £3,500 in today's money), which was ring-fenced for the hiring and payment of a technical adviser. There was even £5 from an unnamed person in Brazil, who had heard a BBC broadcast about the children's allotment in Russia Lane and who continued to give money for the remainder of the war.

Another great supporter was the theatrical entrepreneur and philanthropist, John Percy (J.P.) Mitchelhill. Born in Holborn in 1879, he had been the man who first put Gracie Fields on the London stage back in 1915 and he had bought the Duchess Theatre on the Strand in 1930. There he had built up a close relationship with J.B. Priestley, the two men united by their deep-rooted social consciences. In 1938, Mitchelhill set up a home for the blind in Kentish Town which he later used as a refuge for victims of the Blitz. Its gardens he had converted into plots for aspiring Diggers for Victory, and the Bethnal Green project naturally appealed to him. Congratulating them on 'a fine public-spirited job of work', he presented the Association with: 100 spades, 100 forks, 100 rakes, 30 hand trowels, 10 pickaxes, 50 Dutch hoes, 10 draw hoes, 10 hand barrows and 12 watering cans.

The Mitchelhill Cup was awarded to the tenant of the best allotment and the Association's membership had an enviable record in qualifying for official Dig for Victory Certificates of Merit. Plots varied significantly in size, from small individual plots to others that covered up to 2,000 square yards. Where ground clearance was beyond the practical capabilities of the organisation, the War Debris Survey Department (under the jurisdiction of the London County Council) was called upon to help with the preparation of sites. An impressive model allotment was set up in Ravenscroft Street and used to educate and enthuse new growers. There was a concerted effort to get young people involved too, with pupils from the Cranbrook and Daniel Street Schools each having their own plots.

The running of the Association was not without the occasional struggle. The appointment of a technical adviser was a long and drawn-out affair, with several candidates refusing the job at the last moment and the Association having to up its remuneration package. They finally employed a Miss King on a salary of £4

10*s*. per week. However, things clearly did not go as smoothly as either party would have wanted, and in June 1943 an enquiry was underway to investigate members' complaints about the performance of Miss King and about the use of the Association's finances. The investigating committee reported that while there was no improper use of funds, there were 'signs of carelessness', and Miss King moved on to a new job in September 1943.

However, the successes of the organisation far outweighed any failings and served as a model to other similar enterprises throughout the country. While there were few others on a comparable scale, there were one or two, notably that run by the Manchester Corporation. On 17 June 1943, the Bethnal Green Association received the ultimate honour of a visit by Queen Elizabeth. She had developed a strong affinity with the area during the war, having famously declared in the aftermath of the bombing of Buckingham Palace in 1940 that: 'I'm glad we have been bombed. Now I can look the East End in the face.' Two days after the visit to Bethnal Green her Lady-in-Waiting wrote to the chairman, commenting that 'The Queen will never forget the good work that Her Majesty saw being done ...'.

The enterprise was necessarily one designed to thrive amid the hardship of wartime but was unsustainable during peace. When the war was over, it was essential that the area began the process of rebuilding, with housing clearly a far more pressing need than the maintenance of allotments. Although it must have been a wrench for some of those gardeners to see their plots taken from them and destroyed at the war's end, it was an inevitability that the Association accepted. As early as 1944, it used its official report to predict that once Germany had been defeated, '80 per cent of the work of the Association would come to an end' and only some fifty plots would be kept going.

In August 1944 Woolton's successor at the Ministry of Food, John Llewellin, acknowledged how much was owed by the capital to its growers: 'But there is one thing about which little has been said which has helped London to remain staunch and steadfast. Londoners have been fed. Not enough praise has been given to those who played a part in doing this.' Bethnal Green's special triumph in building something so thriving, productive and uniting from the rubble of bombed-out neighbourhoods was celebrated in a note from the Duke of Norfolk, Parliamentary Secretary to the Ministry of Agriculture. On 15 October 1942, he wrote:

> The Bethnal Green Bombed Sites (Producers') Association is one of the most heartening results of the 'Dig for Victory' campaign. Here we have a group of people who have suffered an ordeal more terrible than had ever been endured before by the civilian population in this country. Yet in spite of this you have turned devastation to good account by sheer dint of hard work and determination. This is a story that will live for a very long time.

Within a few short weeks of the Duke's letter, news came of Montgomery's victory over the Axis forces at El Alamein in North Africa. In a speech at the Lord Mayor's Luncheon at Mansion House on 10 November 1942, Churchill commented: 'Now this is not the end. It is not even the beginning of the end. but it is, perhaps, the end of the beginning.' Later, in Volume 4 of *The Second World War* published in 1951, he recounted: 'It may almost be said, "Before Alamein we never had a victory. After Alamein we never had a defeat."'

The war was about to enter a decisive new phase. Victory seemed not merely a possibility but a likelihood. The Dig for Victory campaign, meanwhile, was at its very peak of effectiveness.

15. Grow Your Own!

It is one of the enduring legends of the war that at their darkest hour, the people of the United Kingdom were united by a unique spirit of mutual cooperation and friendship – the much-heralded 'Blitz spirit'. The word 'legend' is used here advisedly – others would call it a myth instead, a propagandist creation of the type discussed by Angus Calder in his work *The Myth of the Blitz*. The reality lies, as so often, somewhere in the middle ground between the true believers and the debunkers. Doubtless, the dark threat posed by long years of war brought a response from the people that has rarely been seen throughout the nation's long history. Aside from tales of outright heroism, there are many more stories of simple stoicism and common decency that withstand repetition. As we have seen, the Dig for Victory campaign itself casts a light on many of the more admirable characteristics of the British psyche, but where there is light, there must also be darkness, for one cannot exist without the other.

This may have been a time when, in general, friends and neighbours could trust that they would look out for one another. Quite probably, as the old cliché goes, you could happily leave your back door open without fear of being robbed or worse. Yet the statistics do not entirely back up the notion of a land virtually free of domestic crime. Indeed, for the determined criminal the chaos wrought by war – panic, lost records, a depleted police force, blackouts and ruined buildings – provided opportunities aplenty to ply his trade.

Official figures suggest that the overall crime rate rose by some 57 per cent between 1939 and 1945, a quite staggering figure on reflection. In the five years from 1940, the murder rate in England and Wales went up by 22 per cent (from 115 cases per year to 141) and incidents of grievous wounding by 65 per cent. There were some famously gruesome affairs, like that of Officer Cadet Gordon Cummins who took advantage of the London blackouts to murder and mutilate four girls.

But the real growth area for the professional criminal was feeding a black market thriving in the face of rationing and shortages. The image of the profiteering but ultimately harmless 'spiv' was captured most memorably by Private Walker in the classic sitcom, *Dad's Army*. But the wonder of the wartime black market was that it drew in highly respectable people from all regions, genders and classes, who came to see it as a necessary and legitimate evil. As Ruth Mott, the matronly co-star of the 1993 BBC series *The Wartime Kitchen and Garden*, memorably observed, the war 'made us a nation of blackmailers and barterers ...'.

M.J. Trow, the author of *War Crimes: Underworld Britain in the Second World War*, elaborated on the subject: 'Many people – from professional criminals who realised there was money to be made in adaptation of their usual work, to upright citizens – were quite prepared to bend the rules, in order to maintain what they saw as their usual lifestyle, thus stepping outside the law.' Another, rather more malevolent character, the London gangster Billy Hill, became a specialist in supplying dodgy food and petrol in the war years. He wrote in his 1955 auto-biography, *Boss of Britain's Underworld*: 'Some day someone should write a treatise on Britain's wartime black market. It was the most fantastic side of civilian life in wartime. Make no mistake.'

Harry Dodson, who worked on the Leigh Park Estate in Hampshire during the war, recalled for *The Wartime Kitchen and Garden* series, 'I suppose a bit of pilfering has been about ever since man's been about and the sort of people who worked there [on the Estate] was no different to the rest. Things used to disappear and we used to know they'd disappeared and the police didn't do much about it.' Indeed, Harry admitted that he himself had traded a few substandard tomatoes that weren't good enough for the canteen in return for the odd cigarette or two. As he explained, 'There's no doubt the black market did come into it from time to time – human nature being what it is, it was always bound to come in. I don't doubt that if you had a crop and it was only a very poor crop and you knew Mrs So-and-so could handle pretty well what you've got and she was going to pay a bit over the odds, then yes no doubt it would slip through.' One young girl witnessed how even officialdom could be persuaded into a little light corruption, remembering how her father, who kept pigs, could persuade the man from the Ministry to note down a lower figure than the number of animals he had actually slaughtered in exchange for a few prime cuts.

By the end of the war, the justice system had heard some 114,000 cases of black marketeering. In 1943, there was a case in which 5 million clothing coupons were stolen. Even the great and the good could find themselves embroiled. Ivor Novello, the composer of such patriotic songs as 'Keep the Home Fires Burning' and 'Rose of England', served half of an eight-week sentence for the misuse of petrol coupons.

While it would be a gross overstatement to say that the back gardens and allotments of Britain became hotbeds of nefarious goings-on, they were by no means exempt from the odd shady activity. As Mr Middleton once noted, his tongue gently planted in cheek: 'Gardeners are bigger liars than fishermen. Gardeners like to swank to one another.' As anyone who has ever spent any length of time at a horticultural show will know, they are also by nature a competitive lot. A humorous editorial in *The Times* on 1 September 1942 probed the subject:

> The Minister of Agriculture, or whoever first urged the public to dig for victory, must to-day be the happiest of mortals; everywhere he gets oral evidence that all and sundry have followed his wise precept. We are all gardeners now … The Minister must have known that what would begin as a duty, a piece of necessary but rather dull war work, would rapidly grow into an absorbing pleasure … Many coming to it [gardening] for the first time have discovered, somewhat to their surprise, that it is a singularly fertile seed-bed of professional jealousy … Beneath the amiable horticultural exchanges now to be heard in clubs, restaurants, and city offices the heat of hidden fires may be felt … There is in gardening a great deal of what golfers know as 'beginner's luck'. Some beginners can break all the rules, fail to rotate their crops, set something that needs sun where it is more likely to catch the wind and yet produce results at which experts gape with blank green-eyed amazement. On such occasions nobody can reasonably be expected to behave well.

The pursuit of a 'First Place' in the giant marrow category at the local horticultural show has no doubt prompted many an incident of illicit sabotage over the years, and that sort of business almost certainly carried on unimpeded. But the upsurge in *criminal* behaviour affecting Diggers for Victory took two main forms: mindless vandalism and calculated plundering.

Thankfully, most growers emerged from the war untroubled by either. A Ministry of Agriculture survey conducted in the autumn of 1942 showed that 58.9 per cent of respondents had experienced no difficulties of any sort (whether it be administrative, practical, anti-social or criminal) since signing up to the campaign. Just 1.2 per cent voiced a concern about stolen vegetables. A not uncommon complaint was, though, voiced by one gardener – the 'failure of local authorities to provide adequate fences to keep children and rabbits away'.

Few things could be more disheartening for a grower than to turn up at their plot to discover some thoughtless oik had undone untold amounts of hard work. Unfortunately, the rapid expansion of the Dig for Victory movement, coupled with declining numbers of police, who were often occupied with other, more pressing matters, left many gardens and allotments vulnerable and – because of the need to make the best use of materials in short supply – often unfenced.

On 25 May 1943, Major Guy Lloyd, the MP for Renfrewshire East, raised just this issue and its unwanted consequences. He asked the Parliamentary Secretary to the Ministry of Works if he was aware that 'the regulations of his Department, by the removal of the railings which divide back gardens in Renfrewshire, result in serious damage to planted vegetable gardens by the engines of removal and exposure to depredation by dogs and children, thereby handicapping those who are responding to the "Dig for Victory" campaign ...'.

It was an issue that had occupied the attentions of the Bethnal Green Association too, its minutes recording that in July 1942, 'Miss Leverson reported that considerable difficulty had been experiences with the site Nos. 57/65, Russia Lane, which had been worked by schoolboys and herself, owing to stealing and destructiveness ...'.

In May 1942, the BBC broadcaster Roy Hay had been alerted to an incident suffered by a colleague at the Ministry of Agriculture, who could at least see the funny side of an event that turned into high farce:

You may remember that a week or two ago we had a chat in the restaurant about the damage done to allotments by dogs and small boys. I have had another experience of this in the last two or three days. While I know the law is supposed to give one protection, it seems to me that it doesn't work because of the difficulties of catching your dog, policeman and creditable witness all at the same time. Would it be a good idea, do you think, to get the Ministry to ask for a postscript period after the News one night in which to 'plug' this matter, which is even more important now that seedlings are coming along.

The other morning I noticed a couple of dogs having a fine game in the middle of my peas. I wasn't dressed, but I rushed across the road in my pyjamas, carpet slippers and a pullover and after a desperate chase, cornered the larger one and administered a good whacking. I was able to identify the beast and had quite a satisfactory talk with the owner later in the morning. The smaller of the two escaped me entirely though I know it well by sight and, I believe it to be – worse and worse – the property of a policeman. Something really must be done. I am even willing to let you interview me on what it feels like to run about an allotment in pyjamas and carpet slippers!

The BBC was, in truth, not overly keen in getting heavily into the issue. When the Ministry of Agriculture wrote to suggest that its news bulletins might include more stories warning against pilfering, the suggestion was politely rejected on the grounds that judgements coming weeks or months after the original crime rendered them un-newsworthy. One suspects the BBC had a point. Set against the many other events of the war that could be reported upon, talk of ravaged brassicas did indeed lack dramatic punch.

Christine Burdekin (née Wells) though, remembered an incident in which an act of minor vandalism somehow only serves to warm the heart. Christine spent much time with her sister Kathleen and her mother on the family allotment, which her uncle Frank, who was in a reserved occupation, helped them work. In 1941, when she was aged eight, Christine succumbed to temptation:

It was getting near dusk and no other allotment holders were in sight. I had observed that a blemish on a marrow would callus over and grow with the marrow. This knowledge came to me shortly after a boy at school had told me that 'bugger' was a bad word. To this day, I don't really know why I did it, but, taking a safety pin that was holding up a torn coat hem, I scratched that word onto a medium-sized marrow growing happily nearby but, devious little thing that I was, I did it on the underside of the marrow, so it would not be seen until the time came to cut it. Not being very good at spelling in those days, I spelt the word 'buger'. Nobody ever said anything, so I suppose you might say I'd got away with it, but it hung heavy on my conscience. Eventually I told my mother that I had scratched 'something rude' on the underside of a marrow. I'll never forget her words: 'They might have been saving it for the Harvest Festival.'

While there could be little justification for destroying or disrupting someone else's hard work, the motivations behind those thieving from plots and gardens were less clear-cut. Some were spurred on by pure greed, others by a streak of mischievousness, yet more by petty jealousies, while a proportion, we may suspect, were driven through desperation.

There was a very wide gap between, say, the case reported in the *Evening Standard* in November 1939 of a lorry carrying six tons of potatoes in hundredweight bags that vanished en route between Wisbech in Cambridgeshire and Covent Garden, and an incident a gardener experienced early one morning, when he found a young girl from a neighbouring family pulling up his prize carrots, breaking off the big part of the root, and then burying the tops back in the earth. And who knows what lay behind the theft of twenty-five rabbits stolen from their hutches on a site in Bethnal Green in July 1943?

But ultimately, theft is theft and the authorities were forced to get to grips with the situation. Some plots arranged their own system of 'watchers', who would keep a round-the-clock eye on goings-on, but often such measures were simply impractical. In 1942, the Ministry of Agriculture issued allotment associations with official posters warning against theft from plots. That was followed in the summer of 1943 by a new Defence Regulation (Trespass on Growing Crops), which saw allotments kitted out with warning signs stating that trespassers would be subject to an on-the-spot fine of £50 (over £1,400 today). The Minister, Rob Hudson, told the Commons on 14 July why he believed the move was necessary:

> ... it is a regrettable fact that pilfering and damage, both malicious and involuntary, have been on the upgrade, and I have been receiving letters from all over the country in increasing numbers. After all, as part of this 'Dig for Victory' campaign we have taken vacant building plots scattered throughout towns and turned them into allotments. There is no fencing or anything, but everyone must know and recognise when a piece of ground is being cultivated. It may not be easy to define what an allotment is, but it is like an elephant – you recognise it when you see it. We want to make it abundantly clear to the public at large that for the period of the emergency, that ground is the property of the man who works it. The object of this is to serve with a notice to all and sundry that an allotment belongs to the person who is working the land and also to his family.
>
> I would like to read one letter from a serving naval rating: 'It is precious little my wife has bought in two years and she is rightly proud of it, for with a number of people making every effort to support themselves, the remaining agricultural produce in the country will go round better amongst those who are unable to do anything like that. But there is a fly in the ointment and that fly is becoming a nasty sore. Stealing from allotments. It is a nasty business. It doesn't begin and end there. Many of us would willingly give to those who are needy, but to have produce stolen is disheartening. Can nothing be done to deter this type of criminal? The devil take those who are too tired and lazy to ever do anything except invent excuses for doing nothing.'

The Home Secretary sent a circular to all chief constables advising that discretion should be the watchword in the matter, and that the regulation should not be enforced against anyone who could reasonably explain their presence on an allotment site. But it was not enough to placate some opponents, who considered it an outrageous attack on civil liberties. One such, Herbert Williams, the MP for Croydon South, responded to Hudson in the Commons:

> Take the peace-time law before the Defence Regulation. Trespass was not a criminal offence. It was a civil offence against the person who owned the land. The person who owned the land could ask a person to withdraw, and if he failed he was entitled to use reasonable force for the purpose of removing him from the land. If he resisted he committed an assault, on which a summons could be taken out against him for assault. But it was not presumed that because a man was on land which was not his own he was about to commit a crime. Now the presumption is that he is about to commit a crime – the crime of theft – and for that reason you have made it a crime for him to be on the allotment. It is no good hon. Members making charges and getting excited over 'Dig for Victory' and sentiment. You are turning every person who goes for a country stroll into a potential criminal in the sense that he can be charged.

When asked to elaborate further, Williams related a personal experience:

> On Sunday afternoon I went for a stroll past one of the allotments in our park to which the Minister has referred. I saw two people digging for victory with enthusiasm, and I exercised

the Briton's right of watching other people work ... As I was
walking past the allotment I stopped to watch the operations,
and at that moment a constable came along, and I engaged him
in conversation. I said to him, 'Do you know that if I walked from
this pavement on to that path you could possibly issue a summons
against me?' The policeman said, 'A summons in respect of
trespass? Trespass is a civil matter.' I said, 'It was, but it is not
now,' and he replied, 'What is happening to our liberties?' This
was the instinctive reaction of a normal citizen who happened to
be a Metropolitan policeman. When I told him what the law was
he expressed great surprise. My hon. Friend the Member for
Elland (Mr Levy) raised the question, 'When are you trespassing
on an allotment?' You are trespassing when you walk on a path
dividing allotments because you are in the allotment area. If I
went on to a path, I pointed out to the constable it would be his
duty to find out why I was there, on the ground that I had no
right to be there, and he would have to exercise his judgment as
to whether the reasons I gave him were reasonable or not. If he
thought they were not, it would be his duty to report me to his
superior for a summons to be issued, and I should be under the
obligation of defending myself and proving to the magistrate that
my business there was reasonable.

There is no evidence that anyone simply wiling away the day
on an allotment that was not theirs ever went before a judge,
but in cases of proven theft, sentencing could be draconian. It
was not quite a return to the days of transportation for thieving
a loaf of bread, but at times sailed close. As the war progressed,
there was a definite hardening amongst some members of the
judiciary against even low-level crime. In August 1941, Peter
Hulme, a 52-year-old miner from Tyldesley in Lancashire, was

sent to prison for a week for the theft of two cabbages and eight onions from an allotment. The magistrate, Sir Harry Speakman, condemned the offence as 'no better than looting'. In 1942, when sentencing six women for petty pilfering, a south London judge described their crimes in his summing-up as 'a form of petty treason in wartime'.

Nor was it unusual for women to be before the bench on such charges. In Southend in August 1940, there was the case of a 39-year-old woman, Gwendoline Walton, described as of good position and education, who had stolen growing onions, pears, and a marrow, worth 3s. from a garden in the company of her 16-year-old daughter and another woman, Violet Masters, aged 50. They had then driven off with their plunder. They were said to have used a motorcar to take the goods away but when the special constable who occupied the garden reported the theft, he was abused by the husbands of the two older women. Detective Inspector Harris told the court: 'There are a large number of empty houses in the town and people are going into gardens stripping them of vegetables and fruit without making any enquiries regarding ownership.'

Other defendants emerged far more sympathetically. For instance, in 1941 a man from New Bradwell in Buckinghamshire pleaded guilty to the theft of sixpence worth of pig food from a salvage bin that belonged to Wolverton Urban District Council. In mitigation he explained he had taken two pieces of bread, which he then produced in court, in order to feed his rabbits. He was fined £1 3s. In another case the same year, a market gardener was imprisoned after declining as a matter of principle to pay a fine levied when he refused to dig up his strawberry plot and replace it with cabbages. Meanwhile, a man from Penrhyn received a hefty two months' hard labour for stealing some potatoes and onions from a railway embankment allotment.

Yet the National Allotment Society still considered the approach too softly-softly, and in 1942 passed a resolution criticising what they considered were the light sentences received for allotment theft. Whether or not it had any material effect on sentencing is doubtful (although one Belfast judge made reference to their concerns) but in the months that followed the resolution, a series of harsh terms were handed out. In September 1942 in Wimbledon, Ernest George Blatchford, forty-four, of no occupation and no fixed address, received the maximum of one month's hard labour for pinching 3 lbs of onions from a council allotment. The following month a man in Ipswich got the same for a haul worth less than 2s. January 1943 and William Lansdown of Bath, a man with an allotment of his own, got a month for the theft of 1s. of vegetables from a neighbour's plot. (Was that a case, one might wonder, of horticultural show envy?). Later in the year, a farmer in Wales was hit with a fine of £20 (over £500 in modern money) for allowing his sheep to eat a crop of winter vegetables.

Curiously, Oswald Moseley, the much-reviled leader of the British Union of Fascists, was actually brought to Dig for Victory by a spell in prison. Interned in 1940 under Defence Regulation 18B as a Nazi sympathiser, he spent several years nurturing a small vegetable plot within the walls of Holloway prison.

16. Do Not Rest on Your Spades

After the decisive battles of El Alamein in the North African Campaign in 1942, Germany suffered a series of debilitating defeats: 1943 saw Nazi surrender at Stalingrad and comprehensive defeat in North Africa, along with the collapse of Italy. By the time of the D-Day landings in June 1944, the United Kingdom was beginning to consider its post-war future.

In such circumstances, it was hardly surprising that the execution of Dig for Victory lost some of its intensity. In addition, many growers were suffering from physical tiredness after their extraordinary exploits, and no doubt saw the upturn in the nation's military fortunes as a cue to ease up at least a little on their vegetable plots. One Mr Hendry recalled his own sense of weariness as he marvelled at his father's ongoing dedication to the cause. The two men shared the family plot after Hendry Jnr returned from serving in the Forces: 'Father had to walk a mile-and-three-quarters to and from the allotment. I wonder how he done it. It was a drudge wheelbarrowing all your tools up there and back every day. And sometimes it was pouring with rain.'

Looking ahead to the prospects of Dig for Victory in the

period 1943–4, the Ministry of Information had correctly identified that, 'the problem is one of maintaining existing enthusiasm rather than creating it'. (The Campaigns Division thus decided that there could be a reduction in government promotion without any detrimental effect on food production, and at a stroke the campaign budget for the year was cut to £100,000 [c. £2.5 million], having been £170,000 [c. £4.5 million] in 1942–3.)

In government, there was a wariness of complacency and reluctance to allow the garden front to take its foot off the spade. Though in reality, the public had little reason to get too cocksure throughout 1943 and 1944. For one thing, the threat of aerial bombardment was ever-present and civilians continued to endure all sorts of losses. As if it had not seen enough tragedy, Bethnal Green suffered its cruellest blow on 3 March 1943 when its tube station became the scene of one of the war's worst civil disasters. It is believed that the unfamiliar sound of a new type of anti-aircraft rocket fired from nearby Victoria Park prompted a huge surge of people seeking shelter in the underground station. When someone tripped on the small stairwell that served as the main access point, a great crush ensued involving some 300 people, of whom 173 lost their lives. The government and the press colluded to downplay the story, fearing it might have a devastating effect on public morale, with the result that many in Bethnal Green felt they had been abandoned just as they faced their darkest hour.

The following year, Hitler deployed terrifying new weapons: the V-1 and V-2 flying bombs. Joan Strange's diary includes an entry for 23 June 1944 in which she makes reference to a newspaper story she had seen about one particular 'doodlebug' (V-1) attack. 'One has wrecked a Worthing allotment holder's potato crop,' she wrote. 'Within an hour or two he was phleg-matically replacing it with "winter greens".'

The United Kingdom had by no means been alone in establishing a programme along the lines of Dig for Victory, though few rivalled its success or enduring romanticism. It was not just the war-torn nations of Europe who turned to small-scale local production to ensure their food supplies, but states across the globe whose import patterns had been disrupted even if the war had not infiltrated their own borders.

Germany herself had run a similar scheme, an unsurprising development given that Hitler himself was scarred by the memory of the food shortages that contributed to the collapse of the German home front and thus to ultimate failure in the First World War. He had declined to introduce rationing at the outset of the war, believing it would have a debilitating effect on public morale. Besides, the country was well fed in those early stages as Germany took advantage of the food stores available to it from occupied states and used prison labour to work on the land.

But as the tide of the war began to turn, there was a change in policy. With Allied bombing raids taking their toll on domestic production and blockades reducing imports, Joseph Goebbels, the Reich Minister of Propaganda, set down plans for the introduction of rationing in 1943. There was, unsur-prisingly, an upsurge in private domestic growing, and in the keeping of rabbits and poultry, mirroring what was happening in Britain. Towards the war's end, bombed sites in Berlin and other major cities were turned over to cultivation, just as had happened in, for instance, Bethnal Green. One image, reminiscent of the famous photo of Diggers for Victory by the Albert Memorial in London, shows German civilians tending

their crops in the shadow of the bombed-out Reichstag building.
While few records exist to hint at the extent of the role home-
grown fruit and veg came to play in the German diet, there
were reports from British prisoners of war of allotments kept
with characteristic efficiency, bringing forth impressive yields
of food. In his account of the last months of the war, *Countdown
to Victory*, Barry Turner quotes Captain Maurice Jupp, a member
of the Sixth Airborne Division who had landed on German
territory in 1945:

> … every house seems to have a remarkably fine stock of
> preserved vegetables and fruits, and some have home-canned
> pork. Many families keep, as well as the usual six or seven
> chickens, a few goats, pigs, sheep, or perhaps, a cow. The
> allotments are, on the average, much better kept than ours. I get
> the impression that the cultivation and preservation of vegetables
> and fruits has been fostered very successfully, on a very wide
> scale over here: it isn't just the good housekeeper who preserves
> her produce, everybody does.

That said, Joan Strang's diary entry for 27 October 1943 makes
reference to a recently returned private from Hull who was
quoted in the papers saying that: 'The Germans are browned off.
They know they are licked. They live practically on potatoes.'

Meanwhile, in the Soviet Union the number of individuals
tending their own plots rose from less than six million in 1942
to over eleven-and-a-half million two years later. Arguably, it
was the Netherlands above all of its European neighbours that
was most gravely threatened by malnutrition. In 1944–5, a
savagely harsh winter added to the problems brought about by
occupation, low levels of home production and dislocated trade.

Once more, back-garden cultivation was, for some at least, the difference between disaster and survival. The American journalist Walter Cronkite was working for the United Press when he reported on 27 September 1944: 'There is not enough food in the Netherlands ... People are living almost wholly on cabbages, turnips and backyard vegetables.' Even neutral Switzerland ran a campaign. *The Times* reported on 30 January 1943: 'Switzerland has her dig for self-preservation campaign. About 700,000 acres have been added to the area ploughed under, and in parks of Zurich, Geneva, and Berne you will now find potato fields.'

In the USA, the movement operated under the moniker of 'Victory Gardens'. As in the United Kingdom, a similar project had been undertaken during the First World War but achieved far greater success the second time around. Perhaps it was down to the words of Claude R. Wickard, the US Secretary of Agriculture: 'A Victory Garden is like a share in an airplane factory. It helps win the war and pays dividends too.'

A sophisticated propaganda campaign in the US included colour films running to twenty minutes and longer, offering motivational messages and practical advice on how to plant your garden (considerably larger on average than the UK equivalent). One movie concluded: 'No work – no spuds. No work – no turnips, no tank, no Flying Fortress, no victory.' The point hit home; the First Lady, Eleanor Roosevelt, pushed for a Victory Garden to be planted within the grounds of the White House, despite opposition from the Department of Agriculture who, at the time, were concerned that if the campaign proved too successful it would damage the commercial farmers. It was indeed successful – there were 20 million gardens planted, accounting for, it is estimated, 40–50 per cent of domestic vegetable consumption – and, just as in the United Kingdom, the commercial sector did not wilt. Incidentally, no other First Lady bothered with a vegetable patch until Michelle Obama had a new one dug into the White House lawn in 2009.

Australia was prompted to action in 1942 after suffering food shortages, despite its relative lack of proximity to the major theatres of war. Declining imports, a shortage of labour and the effects of a severe and prolonged drought had all taken their toll. Prime Minister John Curtin launched the Dig for Victory campaign in January 1942, with strong support from industry, the press and community groups. Cultivation was undertaken by individuals and cooperatives, with funds raised through the sale of surpluses passed to groups such as the Red Cross and the Salvation Army. The campaign received a boost when, from July 1942, the Young Women's Christian Association pressed for the formation of women-led 'Garden Armies'.

There were comparable efforts in New Zealand too. The government published a self-help guide in 1943, *Vegetable Growing in the Home Garden*, with a foreword by Walter Nash, the Deputy Prime Minister. He praised Lord Woolton, 'whose work as Food Controller of Great Britain has earned the admiration of the world', and delivered a message that set out his government's position:

> The reasons for the campaign to 'Dig for Victory' are so compelling that, on behalf of the Government, I urge every citizen who has access to land, to do everything in his power to supply his own family with vegetables ... We, in New Zealand, must strive by every means in our power to avoid any possibility that Britain may go short of food ... we should be proud to join in a resolute effort to play our part on this vital food front ... In

no other activity associated with primary production is the good neighbour spirit better manifested than among those engaged in home garden vegetable production ...

Elsewhere, the Secretary of State for the Colonies, Malcolm McDonald (son of former Prime Minister Ramsay MacDonald) had instigated a Grow More Food campaign in Britain's Caribbean colonies with an eye to reducing their own reliance on imports (particularly from outside the Empire), to reduce unemployment and to improve nutrition. It achieved some strikingly successful results, including a fivefold increase in crop production on Barbados, from 10,000 to 50,000 tons a year. India similarly adopted a programme, though the challenges it faced were unique and remain largely unsolved to this day. In the twelve months after the Indian programme began in April 1942, some eight million acres were newly brought under culti-vation (about a quarter of the entire area of England). The target for 1943–4 was twelve million. Paradoxically, India was the nation which achieved most in making new land productive in statistical terms but achieved least in absolute terms of solving its problems of mass malnourishment.

Meanwhile, the UK government was well aware that the food situation, domestically and internationally, was likely to get worse before it got better once hostilities ended. It continued to hammer home just how important food production was to the national cause. In 1944, the government released a statement:

We can justly congratulate ourselves in what we have achieved but we must on no account relax our efforts. The war is not yet won. Moreover, even if it were to end in Europe sooner than we expect, the food situation, far from becoming easier, may well become more difficult owing to the urgent necessity of feeding the starving people of Europe. Indeed, in many ways it would be true to say that our real tasks will only begin then. Carry on therefore with your good work. Do not rest on your spades, except for those brief periods which are every gardener's privilege.

Mr Middleton similarly foresaw difficult times ahead, warning: 'We may yet have to change "Dig for Victory" to "Dig for Dear Life". Available food supplies will have to be shared by a starving Europe, which may mean even greater sacrifices for us.' He touched upon the subject again in his *Express* column of 24 May 1945: 'We shall have to find a new slogan, and call it digging for peace and security, or "digging for dinner"; but whatever we call it, we must not slack our efforts: the need for intense food production is more urgent than ever.'

However, when VE Day was declared on 8 May 1945, they must have known that keeping the campaign on track would not be easy. Churchill did his level best, broadcasting on the BBC on 13 May 1945 that '... there is still a lot to do, and ... you must be prepared for further efforts of mind and body and further sacrifices to great causes if you are not to fall back into the rut of inertia, the confusion of aim, and the craven fear of being great.'

But the sense of release among the public was palpable. 'It's come at last,' wrote Joan Strange. Up and down the country there were street parties. Ann Sadler's mother was herself responsible for much of the catering for the celebration held in their corner of Gloucestershire. Culinary treats not seen in years were prepared, even though the pressures on food supplies were as heavy as ever. Over in Ilford, Essex, a young girl by the name of Ann Cairns was dressed up in a costume made entirely from vegetables (complete with an upturned cabbage for a hat) and carried a 'Dig for Victory' banner as she won first prize in the fancy dress competition at her local street party to celebrate the return of peace. There was no doubt that Dig for Victory had become ingrained in the social fabric, but with the shackles of conflict now removed, a downturn in participation was inevitable.

Then the battle to keep the Dig for Victory flag flying lost its greatest general. On 18 September 1945, Mr Middleton died suddenly from a heart attack as he left his home in Surbiton. If he had been crucial to putting the wind into the campaign's sails, his death marked a stilling of the storm. It was not an inconsiderable irony that he was, by all accounts, considerably more adept at talking about gardening than doing it himself. His obituary in the *Daily Express* exposed his dark secret:

> Turn to the right off the Kingston by-pass when you get to the Ace of Spades corner, and soon you will come to a quiet retreat of London suburbia known to the postman as Princes Avenue, Surbiton, Surrey. Its gardens are kempt and gay. But the least kempt and gay of them all is Number Seventeen. And that is strange and sad, for Number Seventeen was the house of the greatest and most famous gardener England of this century has known. Our Mr Middleton ... he never had enough time for his own small plot which measured 50 yards.

His *Express* obituary was in no doubt as to why he was so popular: 'There was no secret to his huge success as a broadcaster. He was himself and he forgot himself ...' The commentary accompanying a film of his funeral in 1945 summed up his importance: 'He more than any other man guided the wartime allotment holders in the Dig for Victory campaign.'

As is so often the way, it was not until he was dead that Middleton's true importance was recognised. Sir Noel Ashbridge, the BBC's Deputy Director General, wrote to his widow two days after his death: '... all are conscious and proud of the lustre which he lent to British broadcasting. We have all shared, with the public in general, an affection and respect for a personality so distinguished in its straightforward simplicity.' His funeral was well attended and, fittingly, adorned with colourful blooms gifted from around the country. Pathe concluded their coverage of the event by commenting that: 'A nation of gardeners will remember him as a notable Englishman.' A memorial gate was erected at the BBC building in Cavendish Place, London, paid for by public subscription (and now residing at the BBC Written Archives Centre in Caversham, Berkshire). Alexander Hay of the BBC Talks Department would later suggest: 'Knowing Middleton's own feelings on the matter, I feel sure that he would have favoured the endowment of a cot or a bed in a children's hospital.'

His obituary in the *Observer* wryly noted: 'The lamentable death of Mr Middleton will be mourned by many who never felt an urge to till a garden ...' Truly, he had brought gardening to a broader audience than anyone else before him. Without him there would have been no *Gardeners' Question Time* (which began broadcasting in 1947 as *How Does Your Garden Grow?* to answer the queries of the Dig for Victory generation) or *Gardeners' World*. Humble as he himself was, he laid down the blueprint for a host of gardening household names that followed. The likes of Percy Thrower, Alan

Titchmarsh, Charlie Dimmock and Monty Don all followed where he had first led.

Unfortunately, having ruled the wireless in an age when recordings were rarely made, the silky tones that enchanted a wartime generation were lost to their children. Mr Middleton, the first great gardening personality of the broadcasting age, was destined to become the great, forgotten man of the Dig for Victory campaign.

Although the end of the war and the death of Mr Middleton signalled a slowdown in the campaign, some momentum was maintained by the new generation of growers who had fallen in love with working the land. A Ministry of Agriculture survey on the effects of the Dig for Victory campaign in autumn 1942 had revealed that 96 per cent of allotment holders planned to keep their plots when the war was over, and 86 per cent of gardeners growing crops intended to carry on too. As a *Times* editorial of 24 April 1945 put it: 'In thus directing interest to the soil and its products, the war has established a link between the Britain of to-day and the Britain of tradition ... the suburban gardener of to-day speaks the same language as his ancestor of four or five generations back ...'.

That was fortunate because the food situation in post-war Europe was every bit as parlous as had been predicted. The collapse of the international trading system was exacerbated by a severe shortage of shipping, making it impossible for food imports to reach their pre-war levels. In several countries, most devastatingly in India, there were famines that placed further strain on limited supplies of basic foodstuffs. A succession of failed harvests resulted in a world grain shortage, with commercial farmers once more focusing on grain crops at the expense of fruit and vegetables.

In the United Kingdom, the end of the Lend-Lease agreement with the USA precipitated a dollar shortage that chronically impacted on Britain's ability to buy on the world markets, particularly with food selling at premium prices. It was a heavy blow as the government sought answers as to how to feed a population swelled by large numbers of returning troops. The government worked hard to refocus the nation's attention. One advert in July 1945 ran: 'Anyone who wonders whether to keep on growing vegetables, now that victory in Europe is won, should ask those who do the shopping!'

A terrible winter in Britain in 1947 did not help matters, with root vegetables all but destroyed by biting frosts, and farmers confronted by the sight of fields of frozen potatoes, leeks and cabbages. Potatoes, never rationed during the war, went on the ration card in 1947–8, and the average weekly ration in 1948 fell below wartime levels. Indeed, food rationing was destined to carry on for a further six years, until 1954.

Lord Strabolgi urged the government to action in March 1947, arguing: '… I hope the Government is going to restore as soon as possible – in fact at once – the "Dig for Victory" campaign. As soon as the weather permits we must cultivate every square yard of land in this country in our spare time to add to our food supplies. Call it "Dig for Survival" if you like, but get the people digging.' Attempts to maintain public enthusiasm, though, faltered with the immediate military threat over. The phrase 'Dig for Victory' no longer held the same power; victory had been achieved, so what was there now to dig for? The campaign underwent a series of actual and suggested name changes, including 'Dig on for Victory', 'Dig for Plenty', 'Dig for Victory over Want', and 'Plant for Peace and Plenty'. None quite had the same sense of urgency or grandeur as the original, however.

Nonetheless, a significant number of growers continued to labour away. Tom Williams, the then Minister of Agriculture, duly recognised the great debt of gratitude owed to those who carried on their good work through into peace. In a debate in the Commons on his Allotments Bill in 1950, he said:

> We launched the 'Dig for Plenty' campaign to sustain the efforts of diggers that might be flagging while we tackled the job on a wider basis on our farms. I should like to take this opportunity, long delayed, of acknowledging the very great debt we owe to those diggers who answered every call made upon them, both during wartime and since then. Their contributions to our food supplies have been, and are, of inestimable value and, I believe, those who dug and are digging deserve the best we can do for them.

He went on to summarise the success of the wartime campaign:

> Every Member of the House will recall that during the war one of the slogans that inspired both men and women and, I believe, children, to give all the help they could to Britain's cause was the call to 'Dig for Victory'. We heard it on the wireless, in all forms, from the bald official announcement after the six o'clock news to many helpful references by the late Tommy Handley in 'Itma'; whilst, until his death, Mr. Middleton stimulated and encouraged us all by his avuncular advice every Sunday after lunch.
>
> At the height of the blitz, in 1940, the Lord Mayor of London invited to a luncheon at the Mansion House representatives of local authorities, at which my predecessor, the right hon. Gentleman the Member for Southport (Mr. R.S. Hudson) put

plainly before them the desperate position on the food front, and urged them to do all in their power to encourage and foster the allotment movement, and so help and relieve our farmers so that they could devote their energies more and more to growing crops other than vegetables. I had the privilege of doing my bit by roaming about the country addressing public gatherings almost everywhere. The response of the public at that time was magnificent. Napoleon once called us a nation of shopkeepers, but it is true to say that in the early 1940s we became a nation of vegetable gardeners.

17. A Lasting Legacy?

The Dig for Victory campaign was but a small part of the story of the Second World War. It lacked the obvious heroism of the Battle of Britain, the drama of D-Day, or the unadulterated joy of VE Day. Had it not been so well executed, it might have faded from memory altogether. Yet it speaks of the experiences of ordinary people caught up in a world gone mad, of civilians living during a war that physically encroached on their domestic lives like no other since the English Civil War three hundred years earlier.

Largely because of the dreadful threat of aerial bombing (around 62,000 civilians were killed in attacks between 1939 and 1945), never before had the civilian population felt so directly involved in a war effort. However, if the Home Front was to maintain its good spirits, it was essential that it stayed well fed.

The nation had quickly come to terms with the deprivations the war brought. They donated their pots, pans and garden railings so that they might be turned into aircraft, they recycled paper for rifle cartridges and maps, and even saved animal bones to be made into explosives. It was said that at Buckingham Palace, the Queen herself had lines painted around the baths to ensure that the household didn't use too much hot water. But a cold bath is one thing, a permanently rumbling belly quite another.

Marguerite Patten, a giant of British food in the twentieth century who did much to mould the tastes and culinary skills of the wartime generation, said:

> I think the majority of people realised that what we were doing at home was absolutely vital. You can imagine if you were a young man serving abroad and you had a letter from your wife or mother saying, 'Oh it's so difficult. We haven't enough to eat. We can't get this or that.' You wouldn't be feeling very happy. We were so anxious that the message could go that we were managing. 'Yes, the food is dreary but we are well fed. We are thrilled to have our allotment!'

Rarely – perhaps never – has an attempt by a British government to substantially influence the behaviour of the public been so warmly received or fondly remembered as Dig for Victory. It grabbed the imagination of the ordinary man, woman and child in an extraordinary way. At a time when the nation's fit and healthy young men were leaving in their masses to fight in the forces, those remaining at home – those too old to be called up, the infirm, members of the reserved occupations, youngsters and most women – were desperate to 'do their bit' too. The campaign succeeded, albeit briefly, in uniting people of all ages, classes and genders in a common cause. From the old man at the allotment, to the child on the school fields and the housewife in the back garden, even the King and Queen – all had the chance to contribute, for themselves, for their country and for each other.

In addition, Dig for Victory appealed to that part of the national consciousness which harked back to an age when the best part of the population was unbreakably connected to the land, reliant upon the soil for daily sustenance. Until the Industrial Revolution, the country had been fully self-supporting in food. The utter reliance on foreign food imports was in reality but a recent development. As W.J. Gibson noted in his 1951 masterpiece, *The Right to Dig:* '... in most of us there is a latent knowledge of horticulture which can readily be awakened by circumstances bringing us once again into contact with the land.' The Dig for Victory campaign offered the post-Industrial Revolution United Kingdom the chance to reconnect at some primitive level with its pre-Industrial Revolution agricultural and horticultural heritage. People were ready to seize that opportunity in droves.

In 1942 there were in the United Kingdom as a whole, according to government statistics, 1,451,888 plots covering 142,808 acres, of which 1,134,215 were urban (90,000 acres) and 242,801 rural (48,561 acres). Such a disparity was to be expected when one considers that the average rural household was likely to have more available land of its own on which to grow. With somewhere between 55 and 60 per cent of families growing their own veg across the country as a whole, the figure for city populations hovered around 50 per cent but rose to over 90 per cent in many rural districts.

Something like half of the nation's manual workers either had an allotment or were tending a vegetable patch. The railway companies provided a further 74,872 plots covering 4,247 acres (the London and North Eastern Railway sacrificing the most land). In 1943 the growers in gardens and allotments combined were producing in excess of one million tons of vegetables. That's a lot of dinners. In July 1943, Hudson said that Dig for Victory 'has definitely made an invaluable – I use that word advisedly – contribution to our total war effort'.

Meanwhile, Woolton had seen the campaign as a way not only to maintain national nutrition for the duration of the war but to fundamentally re-educate people in their eating habits over the longer term. The wartime diet was not one that many who endured it would argue reached the greatest of culinary heights. It was defined by a 'make-do and don't waste anything' attitude that rarely left the taste buds tingling. Experts spent a good deal of their time devising 'mock' dishes – mock turkey, mock fish, mock cream, mock apricot tart, mock bananas, to name but a few – the main feature of which was the absence of the key ingredient. Mock Banana, for instance, was an unlikely combination of mashed roasted parsnip and a dash of banana essence. Yet Woolton and his staff managed to bring the public onside – creating a climate in which they accepted the food shortages and embraced new ideas on how to prepare and cook the little food they did have. Dig for Victory was the best way to get hold of a few extra ingredients that could brighten up any dinner table, with the additional benefit of being advantageous to one's health too. Marguerite Patten considered the subject with circumspection:

> People had better diets by the end of war? That is a comment that makes me smile. Because if you had tapped me on the shoulder, or anyone else living during those days, and said, 'Do you know, it is proved that you are having a better diet than we will be having in 2010?' you would have had a rather funny reply! Because it was boring. It went on and on and on. Do I want to go back to a wartime diet? No. I don't want to be short of tomatoes

for six months of the year or go for years without seeing a banana or an orange. But I do believe those war years taught us to eat healthily and not to waste food.

The public gobbled up the advice it was given. Potatoes, cabbages and carrots became the 'Home Guards of Health' while the vegetable garden, in the words of Lord Woolton, was 'our National Medicine Chest'. There were fundamental cultural changes in the way ordinary people saw food and how it should be prepared. Official literature aimed to encourage the population to consider what they ate not in abstraction but in terms of what it offered to the body. For the first time in any significant number, people developed an interest in the nutritional values of what they were consuming and began to think in terms of protein, fat, carbohydrates, calories and vitamins. There was also growing understanding that these values were affected by how food was cooked. The Ministry of Food instructed: 'Serve a big helping of any green vegetables every day. Greens should be cooked quickly; serve at once; keeping hot or warming up lessens their value.' There was also a popular song to encourage the consumption of potatoes in their skins:

> Those who have the will to win,
> Cook potatoes in their skin:
>
> Knowing that the sight of peelings,
> Deeply hurts Lord Woolton's feelings.

In her 1943 book, *Recipes of the 1940s*, Irene Veal wrote: 'Never before have the British people been so wisely fed or

British women so sensibly interested in cooking.' By 1943, for instance, people were consuming 30 per cent less sugar and syrups than they had done pre-war, but 30 per cent more milk and vegetables. In December 1944, Sir William Jameson, the government's Chief Medical Officer, broadcast a speech in which he said: 'After five years of war we still have a good story to tell. The most sensitive index of a nation's general health is probably the proportion of infants dying in the first year of life. In the last war it rose steadily. During the last three years it has declined steadily and last year was the lowest ever recorded.'

It was a view supported by the 1946 Ministry of Health report, *On the State of Public Health during Six Years of War*, which concluded that its results:

> ... suggest that the nutritional state of the nation was not worse at the end than at the beginning of the war, and as regards children was somewhat better ... the child at the end of the war was bigger, more resistant to disease, better nourished and in every way had borne the strain of war better than his predecessor of the last war ... Nutrition is the very essence and basis of national health.

A Ministry of Information publication, *Civilian Supplies in Wartime Britain*, was authored by Monica Felton in 1945. She gave the following succinct summation of the situation:

> Food, though not always plentiful, has never been less than adequate. If it has sometimes been lacking in interest and variety, it has been invariably wholesome and well balanced in its content of essential vitamins and minerals. Indeed, wartime organisation of the supply and distribution of food has secured a marked rise

in the nutritional standards of the poorest sections of the population – a rise due not only to the virtual abolition of unemployment but also to the adoption of a food policy which has included, in addition to rationing, subsidising of the process for essential foodstuffs, the education of the public in the science of food values, and the distribution of foods with high protective qualities ...

Dig for Victory clearly played a considerable role in this record of success, not least in contributing to the cultural shift by which the British public began to reconnect at a fundamental level with the food they put into their bellies. Statistical measures of the campaign's direct contribution to the nation's health are harder to come by. The government calculated that in 1942–3 food produced domestically (i.e. by commercial and private growers within the United Kingdom) accounted for 1,200 of the recommended 2,550 daily calorie intake of an average man. That equates to only some 47 per cent of the total but was nonetheless a 33 per cent increase on the pre-war level of 900 calories. Bearing in mind that there had been a massive decline in the home production of high-calorie foods (principally meat), that rise was due almost entirely to increased low-calorie food production (i.e. vegetables) supplemented by an increase in domestic animal husbandry. It gives some indication of the problems that would have confronted the nation without the Dig for Victory campaign.

In his memoirs published in 1981, Dr Magnus Pyke, the exuberant scientist who became a media personality, reflected on his wartime experiences as an up-and-coming nutritional advisor at the Ministry of Food: '... figures for infant mortality and, indeed, virtually all the indications of nutritional well-being of the community,' he wrote, 'showed an improvement on the previous standards.' The British people had learned a lesson, perhaps subsequently forgotten, that H.C. Sherman described in the following terms in his 1947 book, *Food and Health*: 'To a much more important extent than had been supposed, we build our own life histories by our daily use of food.'

Was the million tons a year that was produced at the peak of the campaign the difference between victory and starvation? It is not inconceivable, but that may be too bold a claim. However, it was certainly the difference between a country able to endure the hardships of war, to maintain a reasonably varied (if admittedly somewhat dull) diet and to actually improve levels of nutrition in its people, rather than being one where the Home Front was at breaking point through underfeeding and malnutrition. That is a quite remarkable achievement. That the campaign also served as a source of national pride, an outlet for social interaction, an opportunity for exercise and a massive boost to domestic morale marks it out as among the most successful government campaigns of all time.

Despite all these positives, the post-war decline in the numbers of growers was inevitable. According to Ministry of Agriculture statistics, between the end of April 1943 – almost the very peak of the campaign – and the beginning of April 1948, the number of plots declined from 1,339,935 (covering 136,820 acres) to 1,117,308 (covering 107,282 acres). By 1950 the figure was near enough back to a million.

However, those at the forefront of the allotment movement realised that the moment had come to push the case for better rights for allotment holders, while gratitude and goodwill were still in plentiful supply. As early as December 1939, the Metropolitan Public Gardens Association had argued:

There are potential building sites all over London which, if acquired for allotments during wartime, might, when hostilities cease, be kept permanently for the purpose. There is no moment like the present for laying a firm foundation for the future, and, while citizens are now asked to 'Dig for Victory', so should they be given the facilities to enable them, when the time arrives, to 'Dig in peace'.

The government also had its Allotments Advisory Committee pressing hard for increased security of tenure. In 1941 it issued a statement that: 'For the Ministry to allow allotments to disappear by a gradual process of attrition, as was the case after the last war, would be a national misfortune.' The allotment movement as a whole, though, was not helped by the general desire to 'move on' which, understandably, swept through the population. Trapped in an age of post-war austerity, many people could not disassociate the allotment and its produce from a sense of deprivation and lack. Times were tight but there was a desire to live it up at least a little. Woolton pie, turnip-top salad, 'economy pudding' and the like had little part to play in a vision of a brave new world.

Local authorities were keen to resume some sort of normality as well. The need for the mass rebuilding of the nation's cities saw the cause of allotments fall well down the list of considerations. Where there were shortages of basic housing stock, how could the use of valuable land for vegetable patches be justified? The Ministry of Works, for one, was keen to see an end to the plots that had been set up to such fanfare in the Royal Parks. A memo from December 1947 revealed: '... it is the Ministry's policy to ensure the removal from the Royal Parks at the earliest possible date, all war time encroachments ...' The vocabulary was hardly flattering.

In 1945, the MP for Rotherham, William Dobbie, told the Allotment Association: 'The allotment movement will, I am afraid, encounter difficulties in the post-war years, but I hope that your Association will see that the enthusiasm which was shown during the critical war days will continue and that the movement will become a permanent feature, particularly in urban areas.' His hopes were bolstered thanks to the efforts of Tom Williams at the Ministry of Agriculture. Williams was responsible for the introduction of the 1950 Allotments Act and told the Commons: 'At the end of the Second World War, we had approximately one million allotment holders in England and Wales. It was thought, therefore, that the time had arrived for amending allotment legislation to bring it into line with present day requirements, and, particularly, in relation to security of tenure.' Based on the recommendations delivered by the Allotments Advisory Body the previous year, the 'notice to quit' period was indeed extended and a scheme was laid out for the provision of four acres of allotments per thousand of the population.

There was no holding back the changing fashions, though. As if to signify that it was a different age, the Ministries of Food and Agriculture amalgamated in 1954 as soon as the last foodstuffs – sugar and sweets – came off the ration. As the 1950s progressed and the promise of the 1960s loomed nearer, the public was increasingly looking to ways of bringing extra convenience into their lives. Where once there had been the National Loaf, the 'sliced white' now ruled. Fresh veg was losing out to frozen varieties that could live in your freezer and be used as and when you wanted. Increased leisure time was filled not with chats with the neighbour down at the allotments but through increasing use of the motor car or sitting in front of the television. By 1960, allotment numbers had fallen to 800,000.

An influential report for the government of Harold Wilson in the mid-1960s, authored by Harry Thorpe from the University of Birmingham, suggested that allotments were, despite best efforts, once again tainted by 'the stink of charity and economic motive'. The answer, the powers that be hoped, was to somehow persuade the middle classes that allotments fitted into their aspirational lifestyles. Allotments were to become 'leisure gardens'. The 1970s should have given new energy to the movement with the emergence of the self-sufficiency brigade, whose spiritual leader was John Seymour. It was a concept that entered the popular consciousness primarily through the BBC TV sitcom *The Good Life*, with a perky Felicity Kendal becoming its poster girl. Yet still the number of allotments fell, to just half a million in the 1970s, back to the level last seen in the 1890s.

Things only got worse through the 1980s and 1990s. In 1996, there were 297,000 registered plots, about the same number as there are today. There seems little hope of a significant increase in supply, especially given the national housing crisis and the ongoing exodus of land from local authority ownership for short-term financial gain. Nonetheless, the twenty-first century has witnessed a revival of interest in allotments and 'grow your own' projects to an extent not seen since the glory days of Dig for Victory.

In 1998, the Labour government of Tony Blair commissioned a report, *The Future for Allotments*, from the House of Commons Environment, Transport and Regional Affairs Committee. It suggested that allotments remained 'an important feature in the cultural landscape; they combine utility, meaning and beauty with local distinctiveness'. Ten years later, in an echo of the Second World War, it was announced that London's Royal Parks would turn over some of their flower beds to vegetable growing.

There are several core reasons for this mini-renaissance, and it is almost a matter of personal opinion as to which is most important. For many, it is the growing distrust they have of commercially produced food and a disinclination to consume food of unknown origin, which may have clocked up mind-boggling 'food miles' on its journey to the plate. Prince Charles, long a champion of organic production, rallied the troops in July 2008: 'At a time when food sovereignty is becoming an increasing issue with high fuel prices, there cannot be a better time to encourage people to grow their own food where possible. It doesn't need an acre of garden; a window box is a very good start.' Since the global economic meltdown that began in 2007, others have pointed out the financial advantages too, Marguerite Patten among them: 'We need to look at gardens and allotments again. We have another war on; we are fighting recession rather than Hitler. And therefore, it's just as important we save money by not bringing produce from the other side of the world.'

Indeed, there have been several attempts in recent years to recreate 1940s-style Dig for Victory gardens for educational purposes, most famously in London's St James's Park close to the Cabinet War Rooms. Graham Hartley, the Assistant Park Manager, recalled the project that ran from 2007 until 2009: 'It brought a smile to my face when we received comments of genuine enthusiasm from people who visited the site.' A similar project was run at the Watford Museum in 2005 to commemorate the sixtieth anniversary of the end of the war. Its co-curator, Sarah Priestly, discovered in the preparation of the demonstration garden that her own grandfather had dug up the flagstones in the backyard of his Manchester terrace in order to grow potatoes during the war. She summed up the enduring appeal of Dig for Victory: 'People were very emotional about the campaign, especially those who remembered it from their youth. It just struck a chord with such a range of people. That is what hit me most. How much of an impact it had and how resonant it could be for such a wide range of people.'

For many, their interest in the campaign today rests on the question of food security. With the global population expanding by a billion people every ten to fifteen years, never has food been such a scarce and valuable resource. Nor can the effects of climate change on food production be accurately predicted. In 2008, Hillary Benn, the then Secretary of State for the Environment, Food and Rural Affairs, established the first council since the Second World War dedicated to the investigation of the production, supply and consumption of food. One of its members, Professor Tim Lang of City University, keenly advocated an increasing focus on home-grown food. In 2009, Great Britain was providing only some 61 per cent of its own food, down from 72 per cent in the mid-1990s. In 2008 Lang had suggested:

Whatever amount of space you have in your backyard, it is possible to create a fantastic little garden that will allow you to reconnect with the real value of gardening, which is knowing how to grow food. And once you know how to grow food, it would be very nice to be able to cook it. If you are growing food, then it only makes sense that you know how to cook it as well. And cooking food will introduce you to the basic knowledge of nutrition. So you can see how this can slowly reintroduce food back into our culture.

This all sounds an awful lot like what was going on under the watchful eyes of Hudson and Woolton in the Second World War. Today, waiting lists for allotment plots run into years in many parts of the country, while seed retailers report consistently rising sales of vegetable seed and a corresponding decline in those for flowers. The facilities may be lacking but, it seems, the passion has reignited. In 2010, Monty Don, one of the celebrity gardeners who has followed in the footsteps of Mr Middleton, argued in the *Daily Mail*:

> ... if we make the most of our garden, then we have a direct connection to what we eat, our local wildlife, the weather and seasons and a hands-on link to the earth that is healing and nourishing ... tap into the spirit of 1940 and Dig, if not for Victory, then for health, happiness and a secure and sustainable supply of the freshest veg and fruit available.

Acknowledgements

Firstly, I must thank Graham Coster at Aurum Press, who initially approached me with the idea for this book and subsequently saw the project through to completion. Thanks to all the team at Aurum for their hard work.

I owe a huge debt of gratitude to the many people who shared their time, memories and knowledge. They include: Margaret Brown, Christine E. Burdekin, Pat Byrne, Ann Cairns, Mary Chauncy, Elaine Clarke, Pru Coleman, Joy Dew, Betty Hall, Christine Helm, Mr Hendry, Ivan James, Colin Jenkins, Gareth Jenkins, Roy Jones, Bill Murphy, Marguerite Patten, Joan Pennington, Sarah Priestly of Watford Museum, Carole Ryan (Hon. Secretary of Carlton and Chellington WI), Ann Sadler, Joy Seaman, E. Stagg, Margaret Todd, M. Tomlinson and Rev. Peter Turner. For further information on the Bethnal Green Tube disaster and to make a contribution towards a long-overdue permanent memorial to the victims, please visit the website: www.stairwaytoheavenmemorial.org.

Thanks also for the help of Daniella Paolozzi at *Allotment and Leisure Gardener*, John Rennie of *East End Life,* Ben Vanheems at *Grow it!*, Lucy Halsall at *Grow Your Own*, Emma Rawlings at

Kitchen Garden, Kevin Quinn of *Southwark News* and Neal Maidment at *WI Life*; and to Malcolm Barr-Hamilton, Jeff Walden, Ellen Parton, Jane Perrone, Philip Norman, Donna McDaid and the National Society of Allotment and Leisure Gardeners (NSALG).

I made use of several archives. Chief among them were:
 The BBC Written Archives (R34/642, RCont 1, R16/416, R28/114/1, R51/195/1, R30/2, 179/1)
 The Garden Museum
 Hansard, *The Official Report of Parliamentary Debates*, http:// hansard.millbanksystems.com/
 The Imperial War Museum (Misc 171/2627, 08/72/1, 96/18/1)
 Mass Observation Archive, the Trustees of the Mass Observation Archive, University of Sussex
 The National Archive (MAF 126, 156/375, 169/36, 169/40, 169/43, 176/8, 38/876, 45/10-12, 48/62, 48/725, 48/732, 48/744-5, 48/760, 53/136, 53/145, 74/106, 74/107, 80/137, 83/1054, 83/1295-6, 83/1335, 83/1468, 83/1511, 83/2935-6; RG 23/26; INF 3/95, 3/96, 3/98, 3/101, 6/507, 13/140-1)
 Tower Hamlets Local History Library and Archives (S/ BGA/1/1-3)

The archives of the *Daily Mail*, the *Daily Mirror*, the *Daily and Sunday Express*, *Gardener's Chronicle*, the *Independent*, the *London Evening Standard*, the *Manchester Guardian*, the *Telegraph* and *The Times* were also invaluable resources.
 Thanks to Bob, who shared his memories of the post-war pig clubs, and Celia, who pointed me in the direction of several

items of interest; and to Caroline Hobbis, who gave me access to her family archive. Finally, thanks to Rosie, who gave up her husband for the first few months of marriage so he could get this book finished.

Bibliography and Further Reading

A Kitchen Goes to War, John Miles Ltd, 1940.

Armitage, Betty, *Betty's Wartime Diary, 1939–45*, Thorogood, 2002.

Bernd, Martin & Milward, Alan S., *Agriculture and Food Supply in the Second World War*, Scripta Mercaturae, 1985.

Boyd Orr, John, *Food, Heatlh and Income*, Macmillan and Co., 1936.

Briggs, Asa, *Go To It! Working for Victory on the Home Front 1939–1945*, Mitchell Beazley, 2000.

Calder, Angus, *The Myth of the Blitz*, Jonathan Cape Ltd, 1991.

—. *The People's War: Britain 1939–45*, Cape, 1969.

Carter, F. W. P., *Food Growing, Storing and Cooking*, Penguin, 1941.

Chalker, Bryan, *Cook-Ups in World War Two: Recipes from the Kitchen Front*, Redcliffe Press Ltd, 1987.

Charles Wyse-Gardner, *Cloches versus Hitler*, Chase Protected Cultivation Ltd, 1939.

Chevely, Stephen, *A Garden Goes to War*, John Miles Ltd, 1940.

Churchill, Winston, *The Second World War: Vol. 4: The Hinge of Fate*, Cassell, 1951.

Climent, James & Russell, Thaddeus (Eds.), *The Home Front Encyclopedia: United States, Britain, and Canada in World Wars I and II*, ABC-CLIO, 2006.

Cook, Raymond A., *Plots Against Hitler*, Northumberland Press, 1941.

Copley, G.H., *How to Make and Manage an Allotment*, John Crowther Ltd, 1942.

Davies, Jennifer, *The Wartime Kitchen and Garden*, BBC Books, 1993.

Dig For Victory (Documentary), Royal Horticultural Society, 2006.

Dig For Victory pamphlets, Ministry of Agriculture and Fisheries, 1941–45.

Donnelly, Peter (Ed.), *Mrs Milburn's Diaries*, George Harrap & Co. Ltd, 1979.

Drummond, J.C., *The Englishman's Food: A History of Five Centuries of English Diet*, Jonathan Cape, 1939.

Family Diet and Health in Pre-War Britain, Carnegie UK Trust/Rowett Reasearch Institute, 1955.

Fearnley-Whittingstall, Jane, *Ministry of Food: Thrifty Wartime Ways to Feed Your Family Today*, Hodder & Stoughton, 2010.

Felton, Monica, *Civilian Supplies in Wartime Britain*, Ministry of Information, 1945.

Food Facts for the Kitchen Front: A Book of Wartime Recipes and Hints, Collins, 1941.

Gardeners Are Asking …, Plant Protection Ltd, 1942.

Gardiner, Juliet, *Wartime Britain 1939–45*, Headline Books, 2004.

Gibson, W.J., *The Right to Dig*, Gibsonian Publications, 1951.

Goodall, Felicity, *Voices from the Home Front*, David & Charles, 2004.

Goodchild, Claude H. & Thompson, Alan *Keeping Poultry and Rabbits on Scraps*, Penguin, 1941.

Hammond, R.J., *Food and Agriculture in Britain 1939–45*, Stanford University Press, 1954.

Hammond, R.J., *Food* (Vols. 1–3), HMSO, 1951–62.

Heath, Ambrose, *The Good Cook in Wartime*, Faber & Faber, 1944.

Hickman, Tom, *What Did You Do in the War, Auntie?: BBC at War, 1939–45*, BBC Books, 1995.

Hill, Billy, *Boss of Britain's Underworld*, Naldrett Press, 1955.

Home Front Handbook, British Information Services, 1942.

Home-Curing of the Pig and Use of By-products, Small Pig-Keepers Council, 1940.

How to Keep Well in Wartime, Imperial War Museum (facsimile), 2007.

Huth, Angela, *Land Girls*, Abacus, 1995.

Izzard Percy, *Grow it Yourself: Daily Mail Practical Instruction Book on Food from the Garden*, Associated Newspapers Ltd, 1940.

Knight, Catherine, *Spuds, Spam & Eating for Victory*, The History Press Ltd, 2007.

Mackay, Robert, *Half the Battle: Civilian Morale in Britain during the Second World War*, Manchester University Press, 2003.

Marr, Andrew, *Making of Modern Britain: From Queen Victoria to VE Day*, Macmillan, 2009.

Mauduit, Vicomte de, *They Can't Ration These*, Michael Joseph, 1940.

McLaine, Ian, *Ministry of Morale: Home Front Morale and the Ministry of Information in World War II*, Allen & Unwin, 1979.

Middleton, Cecil Henry, *Dig On for Victory: Mr. Middleton's All-Year-Round Gardening Guide from 1945*, Aurum Press (facsimile), 2009.

— *Digging for Victory: Wartime Gardening with Mr Middleton*, Aurum Press (facsimile), 2008.

— *Middleton's All the Year Round Gardening Guide & Encyclopaedia of Gardening*, Shaw Publishing Co., 1944.

— *Mr Middleton Advises – More Gardening Talks*, Allen & Unwin, 1941.

— *Mr. Middleton Suggests*, Ward & Lock, 1939.

— *Talks on Vegetables and Fruits*, Allen & Unwin Ltd., 1940.

— *Your Garden in War-Time*, Aurum Press (facsimile), 2010.

Minns, Raynes, *Bombers and Mash: The Domestic Front, 1939–45*, Virago Press, 1999.

Morrison, Herbert, *An Autobiography by Lord Morrison of Lambeth*, Odhams Press Ltd, 1960.

Neild, Hilda, *Wartime Cookery*, The Star Publications, 1941.

Nicholas, Siân, *The Echo of War: Home Front Propaganda & the Wartime BBC, 1939–45*, Manchester University Press, 1996.

Nicol, Patricia, *Sucking Eggs: What Your Wartime Granny Could Teach You about Diet, Thrift and Going Green*, Chatto & Windus, 2009.

Norman, Jill (foreword), *Eating for Victory: Healthy Home Front Cooking on War Rations*, Michael O'Mara (facsimile), 2007.

On the State of Public Health during Six Years of War, HMSO, 1947.

Oxford Dictionary of National Biography, www.oxforddnb.com.

Patten, Marguerite, *Victory Cookbook*, Chancellor Press, 2002.

Pollitt, George, *Britain Can Feed Herself*, Macmillan and Co., 1942.

Pritchard, D.K., *Vegetable Growing in the Home Garden,* 'Dig for Victory' Campaign: Wellington, 1944.

Produce Guild Guide and Handbook, National Federation of Women's Institutes, 1943.

Pyke, Magnus, *The Six Lives of Magnus Pyke*, J.M. Dent & Sons, 1981.

Rew, Sir Henry, *Food Supplies in Peace and War*, Longmans, Green & Co., 1920.

Rohde, Eleanour Sinclair, *Culinary and Salad Herbs*, Country Life, 1940.

— *Hay Box Cookery*, George Routledge & Sons, 1939.

— *The Wartime Vegetable Garden*, George Routledge & Sons, 1940.

Sanders, T.W., *Kitchen Garden and Allotment*, W.H. & L. Collingridge Ltd, 1939.

Sherman, H.C., *Food and Health*, Macmillan and Co., 1947.

Short, Brian et al, *The National Farm Survey, 1941–1943: State Surveillance and the Countryside in England and Wales in the Second World War*, CABI Publishing, 2000.

Smyth, John, *Trench Warfare: A Study of 'Dig for Victory' in Brighton and Hove during World War Two*, Brighton and Hove Allotment Federation (www.bhaf.org.uk/documents/Trench_warfare_-_Dig_for_victory_for_Brighton.PDF).

Spry, Constance, *Come into the Garden, Cook*, J.M. Dent & Sons, 1942.

Steinbeck, John, *Once There Was a War*, Penguin Modern Classics, revised ed. 2001.

Strange, Joan (McCooey, Chris, Ed.), *Despatches from the Home Front: The War Diaries of Joan Strange*, Monarch, 1989.

Swift, Jonathan, *Gulliver's Travels*, Penguin Classics, revised ed. 2003.

Taylor, A.J.P., *English History 1914–45*, OUP, 1979.

Terry, Josephine, *Food Without Fuss*, Faber & Faber, 1946.

The Future for Allotments, Stationery Office Books, 1998.

The Vegetable Garden Displayed, Royal Horticultural Society, 1941.

Thorpe, Frances, Pronay, Nicholas & Coultass, Clive, *British Official Films in the Second World War: A Descriptive Catalogue*, CLIO, 1980.

Trow, M.J., *War Crimes: Underworld Britain in the Second World War*, Pen & Sword Books Ltd, 2008.

Turner, Barry, *Countdown to Victory*, Hodder & Stoughton Ltd, 2004.

Tyrer, Nicola, *They Fought in the Fields: Women's Land Army – The Story of a Forgotten Victory*, Sinclair-Stevenson Ltd, 1996.

Uglow, Jenny, *A Little History of British Gardening*, Chatto & Windus, 2004.

Veal, Irene, *Recipes of the 1940s*, John Gifford, 1944.

Walworth, George, *Feeding the Nation in Peace and War*, Allen & Unwin, 1940.

Way, Twigs, *Allotment and Garden Guide: A Monthly Guide to Better Wartime Gardening*, Sabrestorm Publishing, 2009.

Way, Twigs, *Allotments*, Shire Publications Ltd, 2008.

Williams, Tom, *Digging for Britain*, Hutchinson, 1965.

Wilt, Alan F., *Food for War: Agriculture and Rearmament in Britain before the Second World War*, OUP, 2001.

Wing, Sandra Koa, *Our Longest Days: A People's History of the Second World War*, Profile Books, 2008.

Wise Eating in Wartime, HMSO, 1943.

Woolton, Frederick James Marquis, *The Memoirs of the Rt. Hon. the Earl of Woolton*, Cassell, 1959.

World Carrot Museum, www.carrotmuseum.co.uk, (accessed February 2011).

Index